PÁLS LEIZLA

THE VISION OF ST PAUL

EDITED AND TRANSLATED BY DARIO BULLITTA

VIKING SOCIETY FOR NORTHERN RESEARCH
UNIVERSITY COLLEGE LONDON
2017

VIKING SOCIETY TEXTS

General Editors
Alison Finlay
Carl Phelpstead

© Viking Society for Northern Research 2017
Printed by Short Run Press Limited, Exeter

ISBN: 978-0-903521-96-3

Cover image: Christ as Man of Sorrow, showing the instruments of the passion (See introduction, p. xxxviii).
Arnamagnæan Collection, AM 683 d 4to, f. 1r (*c*. 1385–99).
Photograph by permission of the Arnamagnæan Institute, Copenhagen.
Photograph: Suzanne Reitz.

CONTENTS

INTRODUCTION	v
Icelandic Manuscripts	ix
The Latin Source Text	xii
The Norse Text	xvi
Sins of the Tongue	xviii
Vocabulary	xxi
Páls leizla and Norwegian Texts	xxiv
Páls leizla and Icelandic Texts	xxx
Christology	xxxiv
Provenance	xliii
Edition and Translation	xlvii
TEXTS	1
Páls leizla	2
De Visione Sancti Pauli	2
TRANSLATIONS	
The Vision of St Paul	3
On the Vision of St Paul	3
BIBLIOGRAPHY AND ABBREVIATIONS	32
INDEX OF SCRIPTURAL QUOTATIONS	39
INDEX OF MANUSCRIPTS	40
GENERAL INDEX	42

ACKNOWLEDGEMENTS

Several scholars and colleagues deserve special acknowledgement for the valuable suggestions and unwavering support provided throughout the preparation of this edition. I am particularly grateful to Kirsten Wolf (University Wisconsin–Madison), Haki Antonsson (University College London), Alex Speed Kjeldsen (The Arnamagnæan Manuscript Collection, University of Copenhagen), Marteinn Helgi Sigurðsson (Íslenzk fornrit, Reykjavík), Stephen Pelle (Center for Medieval Studies and The Dictionary of Old English, University of Toronto), Simonetta Battista (The Dictionary of Old Norse Prose, University of Copenhagen), Þorbjörg Helgadóttir (The Dictionary of Old Norse Prose, University of Copenhagen) and Carla Falluomini (University of Perugia), for discussing with me textual, lexical and translational matters related to the Norse texts and manuscripts. I am also most grateful to the Jay C. and Ruth Halls Fund at the University Wisconsin–Madison, for a visiting scholar fellowship which allowed me to present a lecture based on the present study at the Department of German, Nordic and Slavic in Fall 2016. During the preparation of the critical text and English translation, I have consulted and made use of all the available editions of *Páls leizla* and the *Visio Pauli* and I am especially indebted to the works of Mattias Tveitane (1965), Jonas Wellendorf (2009) and Lenka Jiroušková (2006). I wish to express my sincere gratitude to Alison Finlay (Birkbeck College) and Carl Phelpstead (Cardiff University), general editors of the present series, for their careful amendments of the original manuscript and for an efficient and delightful collaboration.

Finally, I dedicate this book to the memory of Christopher Sanders († 2013), Associate Editor at The Dictionary of Old Norse Prose, in gratitude for his precious mentorship, sound advice and renowned generosity.

Turin, Italy
First Sunday of Advent 2017

Dario Bullitta

INTRODUCTION

I know a man in Christ above fourteen years ago (whether in the body, I know not, or out of the body, I know not; God knoweth), such a one caught up to the third heaven. And I know such a man (whether in the body, or out of the body, I know not: God knoweth), That he was caught up into paradise, and heard secret words, which it is not granted to man to utter.[1]

(2 Corinthians 12:2–4)

In this brief and cogent testimony given by Paul of Tarsus in his Corinthian correspondence—undoubtedly one of the most mystifying passages in the New Testament—there seems to be little doubt that 'the man in Christ' referred to is none other than the apostle himself.[2] Indeed, Paul was not unaccustomed to using dramatic Christophanies to legitimise his apostolic authority when confronting opposition during his missionary journeys. In this case, however, his accidental ascension to Paradise, and especially his evasiveness in reporting it, greatly bewildered the first Christian communities, leaving ample space for theological speculation.[3] For centuries, Christian literature sought solutions to numerous enigmas concerning 2 Corinthians 12:2–4: What were the inexpressible secrets revealed to Paul? What exactly was the third heaven and how many other heavens were there? Did he experience a strictly spiritual ascension or was his body also taken up into heaven? And, perhaps most importantly, did Paul's otherworldly journey differ from that awaiting other human souls in the afterlife? Such metaphysical questions, and several other eschatological and soteriological inquiries, first found answers in a New Testament apocryphon that came to be known as the 'Apocalypse of Paul' or *Apocalypsis Pauli*.[4]

In all probability the *Apocalypsis Pauli* was written in Greek in third-century Egypt and may already have been known to Origen of Alexandria († 253/254), who in the years 240–50 lists a similar text among the

---

[1] 'scio hominem in Christo ante annos quattuordecim sive in corpore nescio sive extra corpus nescio Deus scit raptum eiusmodi usque ad tertium caelum et scio huiusmodi hominem sive in corpore sive extra corpus nescio Deus scit quoniam raptus est in paradiso et audivit arcana verba quae non licet homini loqui.' All quotations from the Vulgate are taken from *Biblia sacra iuxta Vulgatam versionem* (1969; 5th ed., rev. 2007). All English translations of the Latin text are taken from the Douay–Rheims Bible, available at http://drbo.org, accessed on 2 February 2017.

[2] Paul refers indirectly to himself in 2 Corinthians 12:1; 12:5; 12:7. See discussion in Garland 1999, 510–11.

[3] On Paul's visions and revelations in 2 Corinthians, see Blanton 2007, 163–73.

[4] In the following discussion I make use of the the latest discussion of the text available in Jiroušková 2006, 5–17.

official documents of the Eastern Church.[5] Moreover, a third-century Coptic analogue, bearing distinctive gnostic idiosyncrasies and in all probability unrelated to the Greek text, was certainly in circulation among the ascetic coenobitic communities of Upper Egypt, because in 1945 it was found extant as Item 2 in Codex V of the Nag Hammâdi Library.[6] Two different redactions of the Greek text were soon formed: a more primitive and unembellished version and a more recent text, datable to the beginning of the fifth century, to which the so-called 'Tarsus preface' was added.[7] According to the latter, during the consulate of the eastern emperor Theodosius the Calligrapher († 450) and the consulship of Cynegius († 388), an angel appeared three times to a certain man in Tarsus (Anatolia) in the same house where Paul had once lived. He instructed the man to unearth an ancient marble box from the foundations of the building. The mysterious item was uncovered and sent directly to Constantinople where the Emperor Theodosius unsealed it and, to his dismay, discovered that it contained a script transmitting the authentic revelation of St Paul and a report of his otherworldly journey. Subsequently, the emperor commissioned a copy of the document and had it sent to Jerusalem.[8]

When the second Greek redaction became available and was in circulation in Western Europe, the first Latin translations were prepared.[9] An older, longer redaction more faithful to the Greek original was first made in southern Italy in the sixth century.[10] Its text, known as the Heaven–Hell Redaction since it includes both Paul's journey into the uppermost spheres of Paradise and his visit to the nethermost depths of Hell, is extant today in seven manuscripts.[11] A typical text of the Heaven–Hell type opens with

[5] Origen is in turn cited in the thirteenth century by the Syriac Gregory Barhebraeus († 1286) in his collection of ecclesiastical laws known as *Nomocanon*. See Casey 1933, 28.

[6] For an English translation of the Coptic text, see Parrot, MacRae and Murdock 1996, 255–59.

[7] On the dating of the primitive text, see most recently Rosenstiehl 1990, 199–207. The dating of the second redaction was proposed by Silverstein 1962, 347.

[8] A translation of the second Greek redaction is available in *Apocryphal Gospels, Acts, and Revelations* 1870, 477–92.

[9] The first reliable edition of the Latin redactions was produced by Brandes 1885. Subsequently, and until recently, the standard edition of the Latin apocryphon has been Silverteins's *Visio Sancti Pauli* 1935.

[10] Rome and Campania have been advanced as possible places of composition. See Jiroušková 2006, 12–13.

[11] See the list in Jiroušková 2006, 29. The following summary is based on James's translation of the earliest manuscript of the Latin tradition, Paris, BnF,

a brief introduction where the sun, moon, stars, sea, rivers and especially the earth complain in turn to God about the terrible sins of men, such as fornication, adultery, homicide, theft, perjury and sorcery. A multitude of angels speak to God about the souls of mankind and Paul is shown the blessed and the sinful at the moment of death. The actual metaphysical journey begins with Paul and Michael's visit to the third heaven, described as a golden, luminous palace with blooming and luxuriant vegetation and orchards closely resembling the Garden of Eden.[12] They proceed to the city of Christ where four great rivers flow: one of honey, where Paul sees minor and major prophets;[13] one of milk; one of oil and one of wine, where Paul meets some of the patriarchs.[14] The last magnificent vision is of the tenth heaven, where King David is on a high altar and is classically depicted singing the psalms in praise of the Lord with a psaltery and a harp.[15]

Paul is then taken to the profound darkness and desolation of Hell where he is shown a series of sinners condemned to lie immersed in a river of fire, each according to his offence: heretics up to their knees, fornicators to their navels, detractors to their lips, conspirators to their eyebrows. He then encounters another series of sinners and is told the reasons for their brutal torments: unbelievers groan and weep in abysmal pits; the soul of an old man who indulged in gluttony and luxury is constantly pierced with hooked stakes of iron; usurers are eaten alive by worms and serpents; slayers of orphans and widows are forced to stand barefoot on icy ground with amputated arms, and so forth. Profoundly shaken by this unbearable sight, Paul cries bitterly and asks for divine intervention so that the sinners may at least have some partial rest from their everlasting punishments. Finally heaven opens, Christ descends before the astonished crowd and a Sunday respite is granted to all inhabitants of Hell.[16]

A second Latin text, drawn from the first Heaven–Hell Recension, was abbreviated to encompass only Paul's visit to Hell, and is consequently known

---

nouv. acq. lat. 1631 (ff. 40v–48v), written in the ninth century at Fleury Abbey, which transmits the text in its entirety (James 1955, 504–21).

[12] The *Visio Pauli* is the first text to make extensive use of the association of Paradise with the Garden of Eden; see Kabir 2001, 18–19 and the references there.

[13] Isaiah, Jeremiah, Ezekiel, Amos, Micah and Zachariah.

[14] Abraham, Isaac, Jacob, Lot and Job. The image of the four rivers in Paradise is again borrowed from the description of Eden in Genesis 2:10–14. See van Ruiten 2003, 263–84.

[15] On the biblical references to David playing the harp and their subsequent interpretation in medieval writings, see Fowler and Hill 1992, 330–32.

[16] On the Sunday respite, see Willard 1935, 957–83. The theme was particularly popular in Irish tradition, see Gougaud 1927, 63–72.

as the Hell Redaction. This is the *Visio Pauli* (*VP*) in the strict sense, which was, despite its brevity, by far the most widely circulated version of the apocryphon in medieval Europe, as witnessed by its presence in some 102 surviving medieval codices.[17] In all probability, the shorter Hell Redaction first took shape in the British Isles or in one of the numerous Insular monastic colonies in early ninth-century Europe, as witnessed by the first four Carolingian manuscripts, which transmit an intermediate stage between the Heaven–Hell and the Hell Redactions.[18]

The manuscripts of the Hell Redaction have recently been reclassified by Lenka Jiroušková, who has distinguished three main subfamilies, each named according to its incipit: A 'opereret nos', B 'interrogandum est', and C 'dies dominicus' (Jiroušková 2006, 170–99). With its 48 surviving witnesses, C was unquestionably the most popular version of the apocryphon in medieval Europe and the scriptoria of medieval Scandinavia do not seem to be an exception to this general tendency. Indeed, the only two translations of the Latin *VP* to have survived in the Scandinavian vernaculars, a late fourteenth-century Old Danish translation and the Old Norse *Páls leizla* (*PLe*), transmit details and literary motifs typical of the C group that are absent in both A and B.[19] Evidence of this is the fact that, besides the Old West Norse and Old East Norse vernacular legacy, the only surviving Latin manuscript copied on Scandinavian soil, a late fourteenth-century codex from Vadstena Abbey, relates to the C group.[20] Two further codices transmitting a text of the B type, copied in Konstanz and Prague respectively, were imported to Sweden in the fifteenth century.[21] Regrettably, no medieval manuscript of the Latin *VP* has to date been identified in Denmark, Norway or Iceland.

---

[17] The remaining four manuscripts transmit a third hybrid redaction, which conflates readings of the first two. See Jiroušková 2006, 25–35. In the following discussion I make reference to Jiroušková's sigla and dating of the Latin manuscripts.

[18] Leipzig, Universitätsbibliothek (Bibliotheca Albertina) 1608, f. 6r–v (Le) of unknown provenance; Vatican City, Biblioteca Apostolica Vaticana, Pal. lat. 216, f. 126v (V^2) from Reims; Pal. lat. 220, ff. 56r–60r (V^3) from Lorsch; Sankt Gallen, Stiftsbibliothek, 682, pp. 193–204 (StG^1) from Fulda Abbey. See discussion in Jiroušková 2006, 15–17 and 30 references there on the older classification.

[19] On the Old Danish translation see Bullitta 2017.

[20] Uppsala, Universitetsbiblioteket, C 22, ff. 130r–131v (U^1), from *c.* 1370–1400, is ultimately derived from the C group, although it elaborates and rearranges the original scenes. Jiroušková 2006, 129–30.

[21] Uppsala, Universitetsbiblioteket, C 77, ff. 91r–93v (U^2), copied after 1416, transmits a text of the B2 type, while Uppsala, Universitetsbiblioteket, C 212, ff. 1v–3r (U^3), from the second half of the fourteenth century, is of the B/spec type. See Jiroušková 2006, 130–32.

Icelandic manuscripts

PLe is extant in two late medieval Icelandic manuscripts, AM 681c 4to and AM 624 4to, dated respectively to the fifteenth and sixteenth centuries.[22] The text is transmitted in fragmentary form in both. Significantly, in both codices its text has been copied along with that of *Duggals leizla* (*DLe*), the Old Norse translation of the widely circulated *Visio Tnugdali* (*VT*), which was allegedly commissioned by the Norwegian King Hákon Hákonarson († 1263) in the first half of the thirteenth century for the benefit of his pious subjects.[23] *DLe* immediately precedes *PLe* in AM 681c 4to and follows it in AM 624 4to.

AM 624 is a voluminous codex in small quarto format comprising 170 parchment leaves transmitting numerous Old Norse translations of Latin and English texts, mostly of a theological, homiletic, catechetical and moralising nature.[24] Lacking its original beginning, the codex now starts with *Ritning Bernharðs*, a translation of the *Meditationes piissimae de cognitione humanae conditionis* (ff. 1r/1–7v/28), a Cistercian devotional treatise on spiritual ascent mistakenly attributed to Bernard of Clairvaux († 1153);[25] two collections of *Æfintýr* (*Æf*), moralised

---

[22] Unless indicated otherwise, all datings of Icelandic and Norwegian manuscripts and the occurrences of each lemma are taken from *ONP*, available at http://onp.ku.dk, accessed on 2 February 2017. *PLe* was first edited in *En norrøn versjon av Visio Pauli* 1965. Subsequently, a normalised transcription of Tveitane's semi-diplomatic text has been offered in Wellendorf 2009, 411–15.

[23] The attribution to King Hákon, although dubious, is found in the prologue: 'Hakon k(onung)r j bok sinne er ur latinu snere ok let. norena til um botar monnum ok huganar at þeir *fagni. er gott giora' (681c) (*DLe*, 2/14–15). Its text is transmitted in three further medieval manuscripts: AM 681 a 4to (ff. 1r–8v) from *c*.1450; AM 681 b 4to (ff. 1r–4v) also from 1450; and a rather lengthy extract is found within *Mikjáls saga* in AM 657 a–b 4to (on ff. 5r/16–6v/19), which dates from *c*.1350.

[24] The codex has been fully digitised and is available at https://handrit.is/is/manuscript/imaging/is/AM04-0624#page/Fremra+spjald+(r)+(1+af+414)/mode/2up, accessed 2 February 2017. For the sake of consistency, in the following discussion I refer to the foliation of 624 4to, rather than to the modern pagination system assigned in previous studies.

[25] A transcription of the Old Norse text is available in *Leifar fornra kristinna fræða íslenzkra* 1878, 188/34–198/39. The Latin text is edited among the texts attributed to Saint Bernard in *PL*. See Pseudo-Bernardus Claraeuallensis, *Meditationes piissimae de cognitione humanae conditionis*, *PL* 184, cols 485–508. The Icelandic text ends in the middle of Chapter 4, and corresponds to *PL* 184, cols 486A–493C. On the fortunes of the *Meditationes*, see especially Bultot 1964, 256–92 and most recently Giraud 2016, especially 155–256.

x *Páls leizla*

exempla translated from a Middle English expanded version of the *Gesta Romanorum* (ff. 27r/5–43r/8 and 149v/1–170v/28);[26] a Norse translation of the *Joca monachorum* also known as *Viðrøða lærisveins ok meistara* (126v/1–130v/6);[27] and finally *DLe* (130v/7–146v/25) followed by *PLe* (147r/1–149r/25). Particularly worthy of note is the presence of early Norse homilies such as the well-known Stave Church Dedication Homily or *In dedicatione templi sermo* (ff. 19r/20–24r/17), extant in both the *NHB*[28] and the *IHB*;[29] Gregory the Great's twenty-first Easter homily about the finding of the empty tomb by the three Marys as related in Mark 16:1–5 (ff. 119v/17–122r/20),[30] which has been recognised as one of the sources consulted for the composition of *In die sancto pasce sermo ad populum* in the *NHB*;[31] and a section on Mary's Assumption extracted from Ralph d'Escures's († 1112) *Homilia de assumptione Mariae* (ff. 122r/20–126r/23).[32]

[26] With additional material form Odo of Cheriton († 1246/47) and Robert Mannyng's († 1338) *Handlyng Synne*. The first collection in 624 4to is edited in *Islendzk Æventyri* 1882, 26–27, 117–36, 195–96, 307–08, while the second is available at 3–4, 50–51, 70–74, 77–94, 194–95, 204–11, 239–44, 246–49, 267–75. Subsequently, the first collection has been re-edited and integrated with material from JS 43 4to in *Miðaldaævintýri þydd úr ensku* 1976 (Æf). See also discussion in *The Story of Jonatas in Iceland* 1997, lxxxvii–lxxxviii.

[27] An edition of the text is available in Marchand 1976, 109/1–126/8.

[28] AM 619 4to, item 21 (ff. 47r–49v), *c*. 1200. See *NHB* 95/6–99/36.

[29] Stockholm, Kungliga Biblioteket, Cod. Holm. Perg. 15 4to, Item 30 (ff. 45r–46v), *c*.1200. See *IHB* ff. 45r/1–46v/29. Along with AM 237 a fol., the four texts are printed synoptically in *Messuskýringar* 1952, 83/1–107/16. On the Stave Church Homily see especially Turville-Petre 1972, 79–101 and Magerøy 1985, 96–122.

[30] See discussion in Bekker-Nielsen 1960, 99–104 and more recently in Wolf 2001, 285. The text is edited in *Leifar fornra kristinna fræða íslenzkra* 1878, 151/1–154/3.

[31] Item 17, ff. 40v–43r. The connection between the two texts was noted by Kirby 1980, 72. See *NHB*, 81/33–87/10.

[32] The text is edited in *Leifar fornra kristinna fræða íslenzkra* 1878, 154/4–158/42. Section 154/15–155/20 is not derived from Ralph d'Escures's text. See Conti 2008, 215–38, especially 221–26. The source was first identified by McDougall 1983, 75–76 (n. 69) and 300–02. Stephen Pelle has recently identified the Latin sources underlying the Annunciation homily on ff. 118r/1–119v/17, an adaptation of Absalon of Springierbach's († *c*.1200) *Sermo Festivalis* 22 (*In annunciatione beatae Mariae*), and the two homiletic fragments on the ornaments of the Old Testament tabernacle on ff. 23v–24r and 24v–26v, which seem to evoke

The manuscript is missing several single leaves, in the section containing *DLe*, after ff. 140r, 142r, 144r and 146r. The last leaf must have contained the final passages of the text; it seems clear however that the exemplar from which the scribe of 624 was copying was also defective, since *DLe* is followed on f. 147r by *PLe*, the beginning of which is defective, and the same hand would have needed three more folios, three recto and two verso sides, to transcribe the entire text of *DLe* (*DLe*, xxi). The same hand that transcribed approximately one third of the codex, including the beginning of *DLe* and the whole of *PLe*, that is ff. 130v–135r and 147r–149r, has been recognised by Stefán Karlsson as that employed in certain documents written by Jón Þorvaldsson († 1514), first *officialis* in Hólar (1495–98) and later abbot of Þingeyrar in the last years of his life (1500–14).[33] This identification allows a fairly secure dating of the manuscript to *c*.1500.[34]

Considerably more obscure are the vicissitudes of AM 681 c, a single leaf in quarto format, which on the recto side transmits the last eleven lines of *PLe* followed by the first nineteen lines of *DLe*. A precise manuscript dating is more difficult to assert in this case. While Unger puts its transcription to around 1500 (*HMS*, I xii), Kålund and Cahill advance an earlier date of *c*.1400 (Kålund 1889–94, II 97 and *DLe*, xxxiii). In support of this older date for the text, Cahill notes a conservative trait of the transcription in maintaining *e* and *é* before *gi/gj*—which towards the sixteenth century would be written as *ei* and *ie*—but also notes that the change of *vá>vo* and *e>ei* before *ng*, which is consistent throughout the leaf, would contradictorily support a younger dating to *c*.1500 (*DLe*, xxxiii). I would tend to agree with the latter dating, considering the presence of two semi-synonymic verbs *blífa ok vera* in the last exhortatory lines of the text (41), a particular combination that 681 c and 624 share with Icelandic diplomas dating from the fourth quarter of the fifteenth

---

passages of Bede's († 735) *De tabernaculo* and Peter of Celle's († 1183) *Mosaici tabernaculi mystica et moralis expositio*. See Pelle 2016.

[33] He seems to have written the *rekaskrá* section of Þingeyrarbók, AM 279 a 4to (f. 9r–v) dating from *c*.1490, three original letters from *c*.1490 and three false letters dated 1401, 1432 and 1436. See discussion in *Islandske originaldiplomer indtil 1450: Tekst* 1963, xxiv–xxxiii. The false letters are available as nos 121, 233, 257 with respective facsimile reproductions in *Islandske originaldiplomer indtil 1450: Faksimiler*.

[34] See also *En norrøn versjon av Visio Pauli* 1964, 6 and *DLe*, xxi and xxiv. A somewhat earlier date, of the fifteenth century, is found in Kålund 1889–94, II 37.

century.[35] As to its provenance, on the bottom recto side of the leaf Árni Magnússon notes: 'fra Oddi Sigurdssyni mier sendt til Kaupmannahafnar.' Oddur Sigurðsson († 1741) was *varalögmaður* in the Northwest from 1707.[36]

A comparison of the *DLe* text transmitted in AM 624 and AM 681c has revealed that the two manuscripts must derive from a common ancestor (Cahill's *z*) from which they have inherited their common errors (*DLe*, xxxviii–xli and xliv). Although the brevity of the extant text precludes lengthy collations, it is evident that 624 and 681c also agree closely throughout the text of *PLe*. Their transcriptions diverge five times in total: in four instances (40) the text of 624 seems to preserve sounder readings,[37] whereas in a single case both concurrent readings could be considered correct (39b/add).[38] Regrettably, none of these readings finds a direct parallel in the Latin text.

The Latin Source Text

As seen above, *PLe* was drawn from a Latin text of the C type. The most evident proof of this is the presence in both texts of an old interpolation known as the 'Bridge of Hell'. The scene describes a frightful bridge (12a), an allegorical pathway that was in all probability borrowed from book IV, ch. 37 of Gregory's *Dialogi*. Here the soul of a Roman soldier is described in the underworld attempting to cross a bridge spanning a black river that would lead him to the other shore covered with lush fields and scented flowers.[39] Much like Gregory's soldier, a sinful soul

---

[35] See discussion in the 'Vocabulary' section below. The presence of the verb *blífa* was first noted by Jonas Wellendorf, although as will be seen below, its juxtaposition with the verb *vera* as a formula is even more significant for the dating of the text. See Wellendorf 2009, 144.

[36] See *Íslenzkar æviskrár* IV 1951, 19–20. During the first Icelandic census of 1703 Oddur was 22; he is said to be *attestatus* and to live in Syðri-Rauðimelur (Hnappadalssýsla). See https://manntal.is, accessed on 2 February 2017.

[37] A 'declina a malo'/B 'declina a male'; A 'við skildir þessar píslir'/B 'við skildir frá þessum píslum'; A 'sem'/B 'en'; A 'frá sagt'/B 'sagt'; A 'látum af íllu ok gørum gótt'/B 'látum af íllu ok gør gótt'.

[38] A 'tungur væri fyrr'/B 'tungur væri en fyrr'.

[39] The Norse text lacks its beginning, starting with the following scene: A '⟨Ok brú liggr yfir á⟩na ok ganga þar yfir góðra manna sálir án allri hræzlu en synðugra mana sálir ganga mjǫk hræddar ok skulu þær af falla brúni ok ganga sumar lengra en sumar skemmra.' For a Latin text and facing Italian translation of Gregory's vision, see Gregorius Magnus, *Dialogi* 2006, 280/52–285/2. Silverstein was the

Introduction   xiii

in the *VP* is said to be forced to walk on a daunting bridge while fearing its disastrous fall into the fiery waters of a dreadful river, populated by all sorts of infernal beasts. The great majority of the C manuscripts also share other distinguishing features with the Norse text: the description of the soul of a man being beaten and tortured by a group of devils (26),[40] a dialogue between Paul and Michael on the exact number of the tortures of hell (39a–39b)[41] and a final conventional homiletical formula encouraging the listeners to fear the pains of hell and convert to the law of God (41).[42]

Within the C tradition, four more subfamilies have been identified: C1, C2, C3 and C/spec (Jiroušková 2006, 185). Whereas the first three groups are characterised by a certain degree of accuracy and stability in the chronological presentation of events, the C/spec group includes eleven manuscripts, which display a different order of scenes that varies within the same subfamily.[43] The majority of them are from

---

first scholar to suggest this connection with the *Dialogi*. See *Visio Sancti Pauli* 1935, 78–79. However, Dinzelbacher subsequently noted that a similar image was already known to Gregory of Tours († 594), who in his *Historia Francorum* attributes the report of the bridge vision to Sunniulfus, Abbot of Randan monastery in Auvergne, who seems to have described it around the year 571 (Dinzelbacher 1973, 14–15). The vision excerpt from the *Historia Francorum* is available in *Vìsioni dell'aldilà in occidente* 1987, 149–65.

[40] A '⟨Þ⟩á komu þeir í þann stað er maðr stóð við stiku ok tunga hans ⟨var⟩ dregin út inn um kverkr honum ok negld við stikuna ok stóðu við fjándr ok bǫrdu hana meðr járnvǫlum.'

[41] A 'Páll postoli spurði eingil hversu margar píslir voru í helvíti. Eingill svarar þó at væri hundrað tungna ok væri ǫrtalin. Þá vinnask þær eigi til at telja allar píslir er í helvíte eru.' On this particular reading, see section '*Páls leizla* and Norwegian Texts' below.

[42] A 'Nú hǫfum vér heyrt hversu mikit skilr eilífa sælu ok eilífa kval gørum sem David segir í Psalterium. Declina a malo et fac bonum. Látum af íllu ok gørum gótt. Þá eigum vér vist hjá Kristi ok erum þá við skildir þessar píslir sem nú hefir verit frá sagt ok sá er æ sæll er þar skal blífa ok vera.' The closing exhortation is subsequently considerably augmented in the Norse text (41/add).

[43] See Jiroušková 2006, 189. In roughly chronological order: Munich, Bayerische Staatsbibliothek, clm 14348, ff. 217rb–218ra, *c*.1200 (M^5); Paris, BnF, lat. 5266, ff. 16ra–22vb, *c*.1200 (P^8); London, BL, Royal 11.B.III, 334va–vb, *c*.1300 (L^9); Paris, BnF, lat. 3529A, ff. 121ra–122ra, *c*.1300 (P^7); Schlägl, Prämonstratenser-Stiftsbibliothek, Cpl. 226, f. 206r–v, *c*.1300–1400 (Sch); London, BL, Harleian 2851, ff. 58r–60v, *c*.1300–1400 (L^4); Brno, Státní vědecká knihovna, Mk 99 [I. 29], f. 226r–v, *c*.1370 (Br); London, St. Paul's Cathedral Library, Ms. 8, ff.

the fourteenth (L^9, P^7, Sch, L^4, Br) and fifteenth centuries (L^{14}, D^2, C^6, P^6), whereas only two copies (M^5, P^8) survive from the thirteenth. Four of them were written in England (L^9, L^{14}, D^2, C^6), two in France (P^6, P^8), one in Germany (M^5) and one in Bohemia (Br). The place of transcription of three codices (P^7, Sch, L^4) remains unknown at present.

Jonas Wellendorf has proposed that the Norse text might derive from a lost exemplar pertaining to what Jiroušková (2006, 191–96) defines as 'singular redactions', that is to say versions of the *VP* that cannot be classified within a specific subgroup, although he notices that both C1 and the Norse text omit two of Paul's lamentations on the wretchedness of the sinful in hell (15, 27a) (Wellendorf 2009, 129). It should however be noted that scene 15 is missing in the great majority of manuscripts pertaining to the C/spec type;[44] and scene 27a is omitted in L^{12}, the manuscript identified in the following discussion as the closest variant text to the vernacular rendition. Although the direct Latin manuscript source consulted by the Norse compiler is unfortunately lost, *PLe* shares with M^5, P^8, L^9, P^7, D^2 and P^6 (all manuscripts of the C/spec group) a similar erroneous sequence of scenes. After the presentation of sinners punished for adultery and incest (20c), these manuscripts introduce a scene describing men and women eating their own tongues (18) followed by another reading that describes sinners who have not observed fasts (24) (Jiroušková 2006, 736–46). Similarly, the Norse text first presents the lustful sinners (20c), then men and women eating worms and serpents (28f) and subsequently the gluttons (24). Both texts introduce two very similar scenes at the same point in the narrative, describing men and women suffering the same torture, a macabre eating of their own tongues (18) and slithering animals (28f) respectively. The disclosed scene (28f) must already have been displaced in the very Latin manuscript consulted by the Norse compiler.[45]

Unsurprisingly, besides this particular rearrangement of the plot, the Norse text shares a significant number of major and minor details with some of these manuscripts: it agrees with M^5 and P^6 in some fourteen

---

188r–189r, *c*.1400 (L^{12}); Dublin, Trinity College, TCD 277, pp. 335–338, *c*.1450 (D^2); Cambridge, Saint John's College, Ms. D.20 (95), ff. 199v–201r, *c*.1400–1500 (C^6); Paris, BnF, lat. 3528, ff. 14r–16r, *c*.1450–1500 (P^6).

[44] D^2, L^9, M^5, P^6, P^7, P^8, Mk^1, Mk^2, Sch, Br.

[45] Cf. P^6 (18) 'Postea vidit Paulus locum tenebrosum plenum viribus et mulieribus, qui comedebant linguas suas'/ P^6 (28f) 'Postea vidit beatus Paulus locum tenebrosum plenum viris et mulieribus et vermes et serpentes comendentes eos'.

Introduction xv

instances, thirteen with P^8 and twelve with P^7.[46] These shared details represent mostly older and more stable variant readings within the C/spec tradition that have subsequently been altered in other codices of the C/spec type. Evidence of their antiquity is their presence in the two oldest manuscripts within the C/spec subfamily, M^5 and P^8, and the very provenance of the manuscripts that exhibit them. Significantly, M^5, P^6, P^8 and P^7 are all codices written on the Continent, in an area comprising France and Germany, where the C/spec tradition seems to have first circulated.

Besides the agreements with the latter four codices, the variant text that best represents the Norse rendition within the C/spec group is L^{12}, a voluminous manuscript written after 1400 at Droitwich Priory of Austin Friars in Worcestershire, containing mostly sermons, exempla and various texts of a theological nature (Ker 1969, 248–49). The text of L^{12} agrees with *PLe* in some thirty-five instances and eleven of these are readings shared by L^{12} and the Norse text alone. Besides minor details, their most notable similarities are: the description of a deep place located between heaven and earth (28g);[47] God admitting that, besides Paul and Michael's intercessional prayers, the Sunday respite was granted to the sinful thanks in no small part to his own mercy (34g);[48] the souls of the sinful asserting that a single day of respite in Hell is worth more than a lifetime on earth (36);[49] and a concluding statement suggesting that those who hold Sunday as a holy day shall be with God throughout endless ages (37).[50]

---

[46] Only two readings are shared with D^4 and one with L^9. Both codices were written in England.

[47] A 'Ok voru þér sálir í svá djúpum stað sem er í milli himins ⟨ok⟩ jarðar'/ L^{12} 'Et erat profunditas loci (*emendavi* lacus) quasi exaltantur celi a terra.' The reading is omitted by the C/spec group. The Norse text further explains that this region is inhabited by unrepentant men, who had been excommunicated during their lifetime (28g/add).

[48] A 'Þá svaraði Guðs rǫdd ok mælti. Fyrer mína mikla miskunn'/ L^{12} 'Et ait Dominus . . . / . . . maxime propter bonitatem meam et misericordiam.' The reference to God's mercy is absent in the C/spec group; cf. M^5 'Sed propter benignitatem meam'.

[49] A 'Er oss ok meiri hvíld at þessum helgum dǫgrum en at ǫllom dǫgum lífs vors'/L^{12} 'Plus valet nobis refrigerium unius diei, quam omne tempus vite nostre super terram.' The C/spec group does not preserve the comparative construction; cf. M^5 'qui dedisti nobis refrigerium in spacio unius diei et duorum noctium super omne tempus vitę nostrę.'

[50] A 'hann skal réttliga með Guði vera utan enda'/L^{12} 'habebunt partem cum angelis dei et vitam sempiternam'. The C/spec group leaves out the reference to eternal bliss; cf. M^5 'habeant partem cum angelis tuis.'

The evidence discussed allows conclusions to be drawn on the main features of the Latin source text from which the Norse translation was executed. The lost codex seems to have transmitted a text of the *VP* that preserved all the characteristics of an intermediate transmission stage of the C/spec subfamily: it most certainly inherited an old Continental C/spec sequence of scenes and yet must conceivably have been fairly close in space and time to the text of L^{12}, since it agrees with it more than twice as often as with with M^5 and P^6 and preserves a dozen readings that are exclusive to it. It is therefore plausible to postulate that the lost copy from which the Norse text was drawn might have been one of the ancestors of L^{12} that was in circulation in Western England during the second half of the fourteenth century in an area not far from the latter's place of production, the Midlands.

The Norse Text

Besides beginning erroneously in the middle of the 'Bridge of Hell' scene,[51] the Norse text presents the Latin narrative in a highly abridged form. Fifteen original scenes are omitted in total, greatly exceeding the material omitted from any Latin manuscript of the C group.[52] Some of these passages are quite crucial for the development of the plot, as for instance the two choral prayers in which the sinful beg for mercy, one addressed to Paul and Michael for intercession (33b)[53] and a second to Christ himself, invoked with his Messianic epithet (34a).[54] All the more significant is the absence of Christ's descent from heaven (34), a scene that represents one of the significant turning points of the Latin narrative.[55]

The focus of the vernacular text seems instead to be largely on the description of the sinners and their measure-for-measure punishments. This particular attention to the infernal tortures on the part of the Norse compiler can be seen in the repetition of two scenes, originally dedicated

---

[51] The lost beginning included the rubric and readings 1, 2b, 3, 8, 9a, 9b, 9c, 10, 11.

[52] There are no traces of scenes 12c; 23; 23a; 24; 30b; 30c; 31; 32b; 32c; 32d; 33b; 34; 34a; 34f; 35.

[53] Cf. L^{12} 'Et clamaverunt peccatores, qui erant in penis, dicentes: Miserere nobis, Michael archangele, et tu Paule, dilectissime Dei, intercede pro nobis ad Dominum!'

[54] Cf. L^{12} 'Quem ita precabantur, qui erant in inferno, una voce dicentes: Miserere nobis, fili David excelsi!'

[55] Cf. L^{12} 'Et vidit celum moveri et subito Filium Dei descendentem et diadema in capite eius.'

Introduction xvii

to sinners immersed up to their lips (14c/bis),[56] and eyebrows (14d/bis),[57] used in the Norse text to introduce two new categories of sinners, those immersed up to their hands (14/c)[58] and to their chins (14/d),[59] and by the description of gluttons who have neglected fasting (14b),[60] a scene that also occurs twice in the vernacular text (24a).[61]

The most compelling features of the Norse text are the numerous idiosyncratic additions that, much like the above-mentioned repetitions, find no counterpart in any of the surviving manuscripts of the Latin tradition. Several adaptations of the Latin text seem to be explanations of plain catechetical concepts that conceal a desire for greater clarity on the part of the scribe/redactor, and some show a consistently repetitive pattern. So, for instance, when the sin of calumny is introduced, the Norse compiler describes troublesome men who were unable to remain silent while the holy mass was sung (14a),[62] and the very same misconduct is attributed to sinners who neglect to fast during festivities (24a).[63] Contentious sinners who did not hear the word of God are described as dishonouring their fathers and mothers (14c/bis),[64] and the same is said about the soul of a man who was not chaste with his words (26a).[65] This image is repeated a third time and further expanded in connection with malicious men who took pleasure in the misfortunes of others. In the Norse text, they are said to have physically beaten their mothers

[56] A 'En þeir er til munns standa lifðu eftir munaðarráði ok ei þyrmdu fǫður ok móður í illum orðum ok fyrirlétu Guðs orð ok helga trú.'
[57] A 'En þeir ⟨er⟩ til brúna standa bǫrðu fǫður sinn ok móður ok sóru eiða ranga ok myrðu menn til fjár sér ok tóku fé illa eðr ræntu kirkjur ok eigi villdu fyrergefa ǫðrum ok eigi vildu til skriftar ganga né yf⟨irb⟩ǿta.'
[58] A 'En þeir er undir hendr standa ræntu ok stálu jafnkristna sér.'
[59] A 'En þeir er undir hǫku standa svíkja annan til lífs ok fjár.'
[60] A '[O]k átu ofmikit ok drukku ok eigi vildu láta hungra sik fyrir Guðs sakir.'
[61] A 'Þessir menn átu ok drukku á hátíðum ok sátu í mǫrgum drykkjum . . . / . . . ok vildu eigi fasta.'
[62] A '[O]k óhljóðun gørðu í kirkju þá er hin helga messa var sungin.'
[63] A 'Þessir menn átu ok drukku á hátíðum ok sátu í mǫrgum drykkjum ok vildu eigi hlýða þá er hin helga messa var sungin ok vildu eigi fasta.'
[64] A 'En þeir er til munns standa lifðu eftir munaðarráði ok ei þyrmdu fǫður ok móður í illum orðum ok fyrirlétu Guðs orð ok helga trú'/L[12] 'Qui ad labia hii sunt, qui faciunt lites in ecclesia inter se non audientes verbum Dei.'
[65] A '[O]k mælti við fǫður sinn ok móður brǿðr ok sýstur eða presta eða kennimenn þá er messur syngja ok fóru með lygi ok lausung manna í millum'/ L[12] '[N]on fuit castus . . . / . . . verbo.'

and fathers (14d/bis).[66] Transgressors of penance or fasts are described twice as debauchees who have indulged in overdrinking and overeating (14b; 24a),[67] and unmerciful men are said to have been unwilling to give clothes, shoes, food or drink to the poor (24a).[68] Unbelievers in Christ are described in a lengthy passage as rejecting or falsifying simple dogmas, such as the Trinity and the Resurrection (28e).[69]

Sins of the Tongue

Besides reworking material in the original text, the Norse compiler seems also to refer or allude to six additional tortures and capital punishments not mentioned in any of the manuscripts of the Latin *VP*.

The Norse text describes how a man who bore false witness, and many others like him, were punished by devils who nailed his tongue (26, 26a),[70] and how the betrayers of God who forfeited people by means of witchcraft were interred up to their hands and were forced to carry a fiery cauldron

---

[66] A 'En þeir ⟨er⟩ til brúna standa bǫrðu fǫður sinn ok móður'/L[12] 'Qui ad supercilia, hii sunt, qui gaudent super malicia proximorum.'

[67] A '[O]k átu ofmikit ok drukku ok eigi vildu láta hungra sik fyrir Guðs sakir'/L[12] '[Q]ui postea non redeunt ad penitenciam; A 'Þessir menn átu ok drukku á hátíðum . . . / . . . ok vildu eigi fasta'/L[12] 'Hii sunt, qui solverunt ieiunium ante tempus.'

[68] A 'Þessir menn vildu eigi gefa fyrer Guðs sakir klǽði né skúa ok eigi mat né drykk'/D[2] '[A]c etiam eos contra iusticiam oppresserunt et postea cum eis non concordabantur.'

[69] A 'Þeir sem eigi vildu trúa á Guð almáttigan ok þeir sem tǫluðu lygi at Guð væri Faðir ok Sonr ok Heilagr Andi ok því at hann sé af Helgum Anda ok borinn af Maríu meyju ok ei trúðu burð Krists né upprísu hans ok því at hann væri krossfestr ok þeir er ⟨eigi⟩ tóku við trú ok kristni ok heldu eigi síðan ok eigi vildu taka hold ok blóð Drottins Vors Ihesu Christi ok ⟨eigi⟩ vildu til skriftar ganga'/L[12] 'Hi sunt, qui non credunt Christum Filium Dei venisse in carne nec nasci ex Maria Virgine, et qui non sunt baptizati nec communicati de corpore Christi.'

[70] A '⟨Þ⟩á komu þeir í þann stað er maðr stóð við stiku ok tunga hans ⟨var⟩ dregin út `inn um kverkr honum´ ok negld við stikuna ok stóðu við fjándr ok bǫrðu hana meðr járnvǫlum . . . / . . . ok hverr annara e⟨r⟩ svá eru píndir'/L[12] 'Mox vidit in alio loco unum senem inter quatuor diabolos plorantem et ululantem.' Wellendorf notes that a ninth-century manuscript, Sankt Gallen, Stadtbibliothek (Vadiana), 317, ff. 56r–68v (StG [L]) mentions the nailing of tongues, although it should be noted that the text transmitted is a hybrid version of the apocryphon that conflates readings from the *VP* and the *Apocalypsis Pauli* and that the nailing of tongues is practised on men and women, which corresponds to reading 24a, rather than on the soul of the sinful man, reading 26 (Wellendorf 2009, 135 n. 2).

on their shoulders (26/add).⁷¹ The excommunicated who were not willing to expiate their sins were burnt at the stake, tormented on a glowing hot stone, boiled and heavily beaten (28f/add).⁷²

It seems evident that the Norse compiler felt compelled to pay particular attention to the sins of the tongue—he defines those who commit them as *illir í tungu* (26a)—and to provide a description of the relative torments that awaited the sinful for their abuse of language. The first great classification of the *peccata linguae* was drawn up by William Peraldus († 1271), Dominican friar and later Archbishop of Lyon, who first gave verbal sins the status of an eighth capital vice.⁷³ Indeed, the eighth book of his *Summa de vitiis et virtutibus*, written sometime before 1250, is entirely dedicated to twenty-four sins of the tongue, in which each verbal sin occupies a single chapter.⁷⁴ The *Summa* became a standard handbook among Dominican confessors in the High Middle Ages and it is not unlikely that the Norse compiler was, at least to some degree, acquainted with it. Six among the above-mentioned *peccata linguae* may have been alluded to in the Norse text: *multiloquium* 'loquaciousness' (14a), *convicium* 'wrangling' (14c/bis), *periurium* 'perjury' (26a), *blasphemia* 'blasphemy' (26a/add), *maledictio* 'cursing' (26a/add) and *mendacium* 'lying' (28e). To this list *bilinguium* 'hypocrisy' could also be added, although this offence finds a direct parallel in the corresponding Latin text (14a).⁷⁵

It should also be noted that some of these tortures are perhaps not entirely the product of the compiler's fervid imagination, since some of them were indeed capital or temporal punishments that were defined

---

⁷¹ A '[Í] þann stað er menn voru grafnir ⟨í⟩ jǫrð niðr undir hendr ok var lagðr á herðar þeim eldr ok á ketill . . . / . . . þeir voru Dróttins svíkarar . . . / . . . ok fóru með galdra ok gørningar eða fyrirgørðu mǫnnum eða búfé af fjándans krafti.'

⁷² A 'Þeir menn voru brendir á báli ok sindranda grjóti ok aumliga veldir ok barðir með sleggjum . . . / . . . þat voru bannsettir menn þeir sem Guð píndu ok í hǫfuðsyndum ok glǫpum voru ok vildu eigi afláta né yfirbǿta né sǽttask við Guð.'

⁷³ On William Peraldus, see especially Dondaine 1948, 162–236.

⁷⁴ See discussion in Baika 2007, 17–27. A critical edition of the *Summa* is currently being prepared by Kent Emery Jr., Joe Goering, Richard Newhauser and Siegfried Wenzel, see *The Peraldus Project* at http://www.unc.edu/~swenzel/peraldus.html. An edition of the first section of the work, the *Summa de virtutibus*, has been prepared by the *Institute of Historical, Literary and Cultural Studies* in Nijmegen and is available at http://www.narcis.nl/research/RecordID/OND1294348. Both links were accessed on 2 February 2017.

⁷⁵ A 'Þeir menn sem standa til knjá eru þeir sem bakmálugir voru ok gótt þóttu margt at mǽla um aðra munnskyldir'/ L¹² 'Hii sunt, qui inmittunt se sermonibus alienis alios detrahentes.'

in law in the High Middle Ages. As a matter of fact, the text mentions the burning at the stake of heretics once they were excommunicated as a result of their refusal to recant (28f/add, 28g, 28g/add). Public execution of heretics or transgressors of Church ordinances through burning was approved in France as capital punishment by Louis IX in 1273[76] and by the English Parliament through a decree that was passed by King Henry IV in 1401.[77] Records of sorcerers and traitors killed by boiling in cauldrons (28f/add) are especially associated with thirteenth- and fourteenth-century Scotland,[78] whereas in France and Germany this practice seems to have been reserved for counterfeiters (Ruff 2001, 99). In fourteenth-century Regensburg false swearers and blasphemers had their tongues extracted and pierced with an awl or nailed to a pillory (26; 26a) (see for instance Schwerhoff 2005, 142).

Moreover, within the vernacular text there might be traces of two Norse fire and water ordeals, applied respectively to men and women under clerical supervision. These were particularly common in paternity suits and were intended to reveal the truth about an alleged misdemeanour. The aforementioned *sindranda grjót* or glowing hot stone associated with those souls that had committed deadly sins (28f/add) might sound reminiscent of the *sindranda járn* or glowing hot iron, which according to the *járnburðr* practice had to be carried for a prescribed distance without any physical consequence by the accused man who wanted to prove his innocence.[79] Similarly, the boiling cauldrons carried by the betrayers of God (26a/add) seem to echo those employed in the *ketiltak* ordeal, in which the accused woman was forced to plunge her hand into a kettle of boiling water and retrieve a stone. If innocent, she was expected to remain unharmed.[80] Although in 1215 the Fourth Lateran

[76] Formally accepted through the *Établissement de Saint-Louis*. See for instance *The Etablissements de Saint Louis* 1996, 59 n. 90.

[77] The text came to be known as *De haeretico comburendo*. A translation of the decree is available in *English Historical Documents* 1969, IV 850–51. See also the discussion in Loewenstein 2013, 28 and references there.

[78] The first such example is that of the farmers of Caithness, who with permission of Jón Haraldsson, jarl of Orkney, boiled to death Bishop Adam of Melrose at Halkirk in 1222. See for instance Pinkerton 1809, 58. A certain tradition relates that the Butler of Scotland William II de Soulis, accused of sorcery, was boiled alive in a cauldron in 1321. See L'Estrange Ewen 1929, repr. 2011, 30 n. 4.

[79] No other instance of a *sindranda grjót* seems to occur in the Old Norse corpus.

[80] It should however be noted that these were already common practices in early medieval Europe and were imported to Scandinavia at a later stage. The same ordeal of boiling water was imposed for theft and false witness in

Council prohibited clerical participation in such trials, they seem to have survived in Iceland throughout the thirteenth century (see for instance Stein-Wilkeshuis 1991, 90). The punishment of beating or *húðlát* (28f/add), especially reserved for marriage issues and slander against the king, is not mentioned in Icelandic sources until the end of the fourteenth century (Stein-Wilkeshuis 1991, 95).

Vocabulary

One of the main distinguishing features of the vocabulary selected for *PLe* is the abundant use of nominal compounds preceded by the negative prefix 'ó-' to express failure to abide by the Christian law or concepts opposed to joy and delight.[81] An abundant use of compounds preceded by the negative particle has been noted in the prose of *Tristrams saga ok Ísǫndar*, written in Norway allegedly by Brother Robert during the reign of King Hákon Hákonarson († 1263) (*DLe*, lxxxii). A second characteristic of the translation is the curious presence of four nominal compounds unattested elsewhere, which reveal a very distinctive literary licence on the part of its scribe/compiler.[82] In addition to words widely used in the Old Norse corpus, the compiler's unique lexicon can be seen in the use of certain words that did not enjoy wide circulation in the Norse Middle Ages. They can be classified into two categories according to their geographical and chronological record:

(a) a first group represented by words attested exclusively in Norwegian sources, mainly in diplomas from the fourteenth century;

(b) a second group comprising words extant solely in Icelandic sources dating from the last quarter of the fifteenth century onwards.

To the first group belongs the noun *óhljóðun/óhljóðan* (f.) with the variants *úhljóðun/úhljóðan* (14a) meaning 'din, noise, racket',

---

sixth- and seventh-centuries Salic and Ripuarian laws and the ordeal by hot iron is already described in the twelfth-century *Textus Roffensis* copied from pre-Conquest English sources. See respectively Oliver 2001, 43–44 and Keefer 2009, 355–57.

[81] Nine words in total: *óhljóðan* (14a); *ómiskunnsamr* (18a; 34d); *ósǫrr* (26a); *ósýnja* (27a); *ópefan* (28); *óhagligr* (30a); *óumrǿðiligr* (32a); *óverðugr* (34d/add); *órǿkðr* (41).

[82] There seems to be no trace of *munnskyldan* (14a); *blótrífr* (18a); *skjóttvítni* (26a); A *ǫrtalin* with the variant B *ǫrtali* (39b) in the Old Norse corpus. The nomen agentis *hrópari* also seems to be a *hapax* in Old Norse since it is only recorded in Modern Icelandic from 1652. See http://lexis.hi.is/cgi-bin/ritmal/leitord.cgi?adg =heim&h=SigJ%F3nssHugvPs, accessed on 2 February 2017.

found four times in fourteenth-century sources dealing with legal matters of direct or ultimate Norwegian provenance. It first occurs in *Gildisskrá*, a Nidaros guild ordinance extant in a manuscript written around 1300[83] and in order 17 of the *Statuta Eilífs erkibyskups*, the Greatest Statute of Archbishop Eilif Arnesson Kortin of Nidaros († 1332), transmitted in the last section of the so-called Belgdalsbók from *c*.1370[84] and in the nearly contemporary Skarðsbók or Codex Scardensis from *c*.1360–75[85]. In connection with *óhljóðan*, Tveitane notes the presence of the nominal compound *óhljóðanseyra* (n.) in the *Sermo ad populum* of the *NHB* (ff. 17r–18r)[86] and in a letter by Bishop Hákon Erlingsson of Bergen († 1342) dated 7 August 1339.[87] However, the word within the compound has the figurative meaning of 'turning a deaf ear', a sense noticeably different from the 'din, noise, racket within public spaces' (such as churches or assemblies) of the abovementioned contexts in which the noun is found alone.[88] The compound *skrǫkvitni* (n.) (34d) meaning 'false witness' also belongs to this group since it is found exclusively in Norwegian sources from the thirteenth and, to a lesser extent, the fourteenth century. It is seen in the *Sermo necessaria* of the *NHB* (ff. 43r–44v)[89] and in three Norwegian laws found in fourteenth-century manuscripts:

---

[83] Oslo, Norsk Riksarkivet, 50 c (f. 1r–v). 'Aller menn skulu . . . / . . . drækka standande hit fyrsta kiær eða giællde penning firir hvært andvege ok sua ef olioðan ger⟨er⟩.' (Storm 1896, 219/16).

[84] AM 347 fol. (ff. 85ra–86rb). Belgdalsbók is indicated as G in the apparatus criticus of *DI*. 'Enn ef hann byriar edr ohliodan gerir eyri j huert sinne.' (*DI*, II 542/18–19).

[85] AM 350 fol. (ff. 145rb–147ra). Skarðsbók has been chosen as the base text of the *DI* 'Enn ef hann byriar edr uliodar gialldi eyrifyrir huert sinn er gerir.' (*DI*, II 542/18–19).

[86] 'En ſumir menn gera með ollu rangt í guðs husi . . . / . . . ok føra ó-lioðanſ æyru við guðs æmbæte ok halæitri þionaosto' (*NHB*, 36/18–21). See discussion in *En norrøn versjon av Visio Pauli* 1965, 16.

[87] Hákon plays with the assonance of *óhljóðan* with the word *óhlýðni* 'disobedience'. '[V]ttan vaarrar ofmykillar abrygdar þuilika vlydni med ifirdylmande aughum, eðr vliodans œyrum þeghiande vmlijda' (*DN*, IX 134/20–21, no. 117). See also discussion in McDougall 1983, 329–41.

[88] *Úhljóðan* alone is also attested once as a gloss. See for instance Leiv Heggstad et al. 1975.

[89] '[V]ið mandrape ok við hordome. við ſtuldum. við scrøcvitnum. við mæinæiðum' (*NHB*, 87/23–24).

Magnus Lagabøters Norske Landslov,[90] *Borgarþingsløg*,[91] *Réttarbøtr Magnúss Hákonarsonar*[92] and in a post-medieval manuscript of the *Frostaþingsløg*.[93]

The second group includes the compound adjective *forstǫðulauss* (24a) 'without protection', which other than in *PLe*, is employed once in an Icelandic diploma dated 1486,[94] twice in the first half of the sixteenth century in an Icelandic diploma and in Reykjahólabók,[95] and once in a post-medieval manuscript transmitting *Fljótsdœla saga*.[96] The verb *blífa*, a Danish loan word of ultimate Low German origin, is employed in the final hortatory conclusion (41) in juxtaposition with the verb *vera*.[97] Whereas *blífa* is first found in two Norwegian letters dated 1370 (*DN*, I 312) and 1389 (*DN*, XVIII 32), the first Icelandic source to record it is the *máldagi* of the Augustinian monastery of Viðey, dated 21 July 1413, which attests it with the same redundant juxtaposition of the two semi-synonymous verbs *blífa ok vera*.[98] However, as Veturliði Óskarsson has pointed out, this dating should be taken cautiously, since the manuscript that transmits it was copied around 1570.[99] As a matter of fact, the *blífa ok vera* cluster becomes widespread some seventy years later than 1413. It occurs in two other Icelandic diplomas from the fourth quarter of the fifteenth century and in three sources from the

---

[90] AM 60 4to (21va–81va; 98va–100ra) from *c*.1320. '[Þ]a sem huarke se aðr rœyndir at rognum eiðum ne skrœkuitnum' (*NGL*, II 173/14).

[91] AM 31 8vo 13 (ff. 3ra–7b, 8r) from *c*.1325–50. 'Sa madr er lœit hæfir skrœkvithni han er fœckr .vj. morkum silfrs' (*NGL*, I 356/25–26).

[92] AM 58 4to (3ra–84v) from *c*.1325–50. 'En þeir men er i hordome liggia. mandrapom eda mæinæidum. skrœkvithnum eda adrum ferlegum lutum' (*NGL*, II 454/4–5).

[93] GKS 1155 a fol. (17v–68r) from *c*.1700. 'Um ræði móti scröcvitnum á fimtarstemmu' (*NGL*, I 239/37).

[94] '[Þ]ar sem hvn nu lęgi verndarlavs ok forstôdvlaus og j avdn sett' (*DI*, VI 570/1).

[95] In an Icelandic diploma from 1513. '[Þ]etta fatækt forstavdvlavst skattland' (*DI*, VIII 443/10). Within *Gregors saga byskups* in Holm perg 3 fol. (ff. 83a–86vb; 31ra–33v), better known as Reykjahólabók, from around 1530–40. '[S]amt er ydart rike forstavdv lavst nv sem fyre' (Reykjahólabók 1969, 18/3).

[96] In the longer version of *Fljótsdœla saga*, transmitted in Kall 616 4to (ff. 41r–60v) and copied in the eighteenth century. 'Nu mun þad sanast. qvad Iórun, ad vær erum forstödulausar, þá bónde er ecki heima' (*Fljótsdœla hin meiri* 1883, 127/27–8).

[97] A '[O]k sá er æ sæll er þar skal blífa ok vera.'

[98] 'Enn þeir rekar ... / ... blifi ok veri epter þeirre skýring' (*DI*, III 750/7–8, *c*.1570).

[99] AM 238 4to, ff. 35r–36v. See Veturliði Óskarsson 2009, 195–96.

sixteenth.[100] Perhaps significantly, this particular combination is never found in Norwegian sources.

It seems clear from the evidence discussed that *PLe* includes a colourful mélange of terms. Some nouns and compounds find a counterpart in Norwegian laws and were especially widespread in the first half of the fourteenth century. Later words or combinations of words are recorded solely in Icelandic sources, attested from the fourth quarter of the fifteenth century and throughout the sixteenth century. This great variety would naturally suggest a late fifteenth-century Icelandic scriptorium as a possible place of composition and an Icelandic or Norwegian scribe well acquainted with fourteenth-century Norwegian laws.

Páls leizla and Norwegian Texts

In his critical edition of *DLe*, Peter Cahill suggested that the expression *ok brixlodo henne synda brixle* 'and [they] upbraided her with reproaches' might originate from a passage in *PLe* (30) in which seven devils are said to torment the soul of the sinful: *ok bǫrðu hana ok brugðu brigslum* 'and [they] beat her and upbraided [her] with reproaches' (*DLe*, liii). Textual evidence seems to suggest, however, that the author of *PLe* had knowledge of and borrowed from *DLe*, rather than the other way around. In fact, while the verbal 'reproaches' of *DLe* do find a counterpart in the Latin *VT*,[101] they do not have a direct correspondence in the Latin *VP*, where the soul is simply said to leave its body daily.[102]

Dependence of some sections of *PLe* on *DLe* is further supported by the presence in the former of several details typical of the

[100] '[H]afi hér verið og blifið með heiðr og æru' (*DI*, VI 292/4–5 from 1480). '[S]em allra annara yfferbodara skal blijffa og vera epter riettu og settu lómáále' (*DI*, VI 462/9–10 from 1482). '[H]vor vier lietvm svo blifa ok vera hvorke nytt nie onytt' (*DI*, VIII 151/15–16 from 1507). '[Þ]essa savmv vatzfiardar kirkiu vera oc eiga ad blijfa' (*DI*, VIII 162/25–6, from *c*.1507–14). '[A]d þær Collationes skylldi fullmyndugur vera og blijfa' (*DI*, X 569/4–5, 1540).

[101] A '[Þ]uinæst sem dioflar sæu att hon uar þeim iatud hurfo þeir um hana ok brixlodo henne synda brixle ok jllyrda hana med ferligum ordum og slitv hana alla j svndur med tœlum er uier fyrr gætum' (*DLe* 49/21–50/11). W 'Demones autem videntes animam sibi concessam, circumvenerunt eam, et magnis conviciis exprobantes cum supradictis instrumentis in frustra dissipaverunt' (*DLe* 50/19–21).

[102] A 'Ok þá sá postolinn borna sál syndogs manns til helvítis ok fylgðo VII englar fjándans ok fóru með hana illa ok bǫrðu hana ok brugðu brigslum'/L¹² 'Et postea aspiscebat inter celum et terram et vidit animam peccatoris ululantem inter septem diabolos deducentes eam, cotidie de corpore egressam.'

Introduction

latter. These are especially concentrated towards the end of the narrative and find no counterpart in any of the manuscripts of the Latin *VP*. So, for instance, where the Latin *VP* mentions a certain location in Hell in which the souls of condemned men and women eat worms and serpents (28f),[103] the Norse text adds toads to the list of crawling creatures.[104] *DLe* enumerates these three as the venomous creatures inhabiting Ireland, a sentence that corresponds perfectly with the *VT*.[105] The same can be said about the description of men being eaten alive by hounds, wolves, worms and adders (28f/add),[106] a scene that is nowhere to be found in the Latin *VP* but is present in both *DLe* and *VT*.[107] Additionally, no mention is made in the Latin *VP* of the church robbers referred to in the vernacular adaptation (26a/add),[108] whereas *DLe* and its Latin source describe the profanation of churches committed by robbers who steal books, liturgical vestments and chalices.[109] A further detail that may derive from *DLe*, possibly through memory rather than by juxtaposition of passages, is the description of a great house in which a group of sinful souls are condemned to suffer (24a).[110]

---

[103] L[12] 'Et vidit in alio loco viros ac mulieres et vermes et serpentes commedentes eos. Et erant anime vive . . . / . . . alteram quasi oves in ovili.'

[104] A 'Þá komu þeir í þann stað er menn átu forska pǫddur ok nǫðrur ok allskyns kvikvendi.'

[105] A '[E]iturkuikendum ormmum pauddum ok froskum' (*DLe* 4/21); W '[S]erpentium, ranarum, bufonum et omnium animalium venena ferentium' (*DLe* 3/25–26).

[106] A 'En suma rífu vargar ok hundar í sundr. En suma hjoggu ormar ok nǫðrur.'

[107] A '[Þ]ar þolde sw enn auma sæl. hunda bit ok warga slit. barnijngar ok biarnar bit ok leona ok fleiri annara dyra. orma haugg ok eitr naudror ok margra annara grimligra ok ogurligra dyra' (*DLe* 36/20–37/10); W 'Passa est enim ibidem canum, ursorum, leonum, serpentium seu innumerabilium aliorum incognitorum monstruosorum animalium ferocitatem' (*DLe* 36/32–37/1).

[108] A 'Þeir voru Dróttins svíkarar rǽntu heilaga kirkju drápu biskupa ok lǽrða menn aðra.'

[109] A '[Þ]a mællti salin huad kallar þu kirkiu stuld eingellinn mællti þad sem stolid er ok uikt til *Gwds þionozstu er haft. bækr edr messo klædi ok kalekar edr annad þess konar þijng edr þo at oheilagt sie þegar ur kirkiu er stolid' (*DLe* 42/10–14); W 'Tunc anima: Quid, ait, vocas sacrilegium? Respondit angelus: Qui sive sacratum sive de sacrato aliquid furatur, hic sacrilegii reus judicatur, maxime vero, qui delinquunt sub tegumento religionis' (*DLe* 42/22–25).

[110] A '⟨Þ⟩á gengu þau en ok fundu hús mikit ok sá í því menn marga ok alla nøkta ok voru sumt konur en sumt karlmenn ok voru illa píndir af frosti ok eldi.'

The sentence is absent in the *VP* but present in the *VT* and in its vernacular translation.[111]

Ole Widding and Hans Bekker-Nielsen, followed by Mattias Tveitane, suggested that the text of the *VP* must have been known to the scribe/redactor of the *NHB*, written around 1200 in the Munkeliv Abbey of the Benedictine order,[112] and that the vernacular translation contained in 624 4to and 681 c 4to had perhaps a longer textual history than that suggested by the date of its surviving manuscripts.[113] In support of this suggestion, they noted that the Old Norse *Viðrǿða líkams ok sálar einn laugardag at kveldi*, a translation of the Latin poem *Nuper huiuscemodi visionem somni*, possibly compiled from its Old French rendition *Un samedi par nuit*, was rubricated in the *NHB* (f. 75v/16) with the mistaken title *Visio sancti Pauli apostoli*.[114] This seems to be rather circular reasoning, however, since one could argue, on the contrary, that the scribe's erroneous rubrication may reveal his unfamiliarity with any of the Latin or vernacular versions of the *VP*, or that he must have had a very cursory knowledge, if any, of its features and plot.

Another piece of evidence advanced by Tveitane in support of an early knowledge and employment of the *VP* in thirteenth-century Norway is the presence of the well-known Virgilian literary cliché of the hundred tongues of iron (39b, 39b/add)—that are almost unable to account for all the devilry of Hell[115]—in a sermon on the Nativity of the Lord, extant in

---

[111] A 'NW sem þau geingu um myrkuan ok hardann ueg. þa syndiz þeim hus opit ok suo mikid sem hit mesta fiall' (*DLe* 47/12–13) W 'Cum autem irent per tenebrosa loca et arida, apparuit eis domus aperta. Domus autem ispa, quam viderant, erat maxima, ut arduus mons pre nimia magnitudine, rotunda vero erat quasi furnus' (*DLe* 47/21–23).

[112] Sancti Albani on Selja or at the Augustinian house of Jónskirkja have also been suggested as plausible scriptoria. See McDougall 1993, 290 and most recently Berg 2010, 35–77.

[113] See Widding and Bekker-Nielsen 1959, 276 and *En norrøn versjon av Visio Pauli* 1964, 14.

[114] *NHB* 148/17–153/23. The relationships of the Norse text with the Latin poem and the Old French translation have not been satisfactorily explained. The Old Norse rendition is edited in Widding and Bekker-Nielsen 1959, 280–89. On this subject, see Henningham 1939, 43–49.

[115] In the Latin text the pains of Hell are said to be 144,000 (that is, 12x12x100), a number borrowed from Revelation 7:4 and 14:1, where it refers to the Jewish evangelists descended from the twelve tribes of Israel. See for instance Blount 2009, 144–48.

the *NHB* under the rubric *De natiuitate domini sermo*.[116] Subsequently, Cahill has noted that the same *graduatio* is also found in *DLe* within a passage that corresponds perfectly with the Latin *VT*.[117]

Regarding the connection between these texts, it should be noted that the three seem to employ two different uses of the same Virgilian cliché. The reference to the hundred tongues is already an integral part of the plot in the respective Latin sources of *DLe* and *PLe*. Towards the end of the two otherworldly peregrinations, the formula is used to introduce the many pains of Hell precisely when the two narratives reach their climax; that is, soon after Duggall sees Lucifer in the sombre depths of Hell[118] and when Paul, at the very end of his journey, worn out by such macabre sights, asks Michael the precise number of the tortures of Hell.[119] The formula in the *NHB*, on the other hand, is employed as a rhetorical device that adds colour to the warnings of the homilist and provokes an emotional response from the audience, rather than being a crucial passage for the logical development of the discourse. After a paraphrase of Gabriel's reassuring words to the Virgin during the Annunciation in Luke 1:28–38, the Norse homilist strongly encourages the audience to perform righteous deeds during this earthly life in order to dwell with God in heaven, rather than in Hell. In Hell, he maintains, the fire is seven times hotter than any fire on earth and the mass of evil besieging one there is so great that if a hundred heads had a hundred tongues of iron and could speak from the first day of Creation until Doomsday, they could never embrace it all with human speech.[120]

---

[116] Item 2 (ff. 15r–16v). The sermon is edited in *NHB*, 31/24–35/15. The presence of this reference in the *NHB* was first noticed by Moltke (1927, 233 n. 1). The hundred tongues of iron were an extremely popular *topos* throughout the Middle Ages and several texts refer to it. See for instance Courcelle 1955, 231–40 and Cameron 1967, 308–09. Dependence of the *NHB* on *PLe* has since been doubted by Wellendorf (2009, 141–42).

[117] *DLe*, lii. See collations below.

[118] AM 681 a 'Nu k(uat) hann skal eg syna þier en uersta anskota mannkyns og gek þa engillinn fyrir hene og er þau komu at heluit[i]s gardz hlidum þa mællti hann kom q(uat) hann og see og uit at sonnu at þeir er augu hafa megu hier ecki sia. En þo skalltu sia þa er hier eru enn eigi megu þeir sia þig sem salin nagladiz *sa hon j diup heluitis' (*DLe* 74/9–13).

[119] See collations below.

[120] 'Þæir er her a veroldo lofa of-drycciu eða of-fylli. ok vilia æigi til yfir-bota ganga. ok una í þæim ſyndum til dauða-dagſ. þa hafa þæir ængi lut í himnum með guði. ok þæim er ætlat hælviti með dioflum. þar er óp. ok gratr. ok hungr. ok þorſte. ok ſvælgiande ældr .vii. lutum hæitare en á veroldo mege hinn hæitaſta gera. Oc þar er æi myrcr ón lios. ælli fyri utan øſko' (*NHB*, 33/31–/34/2).

Significantly, these two stereotyped descriptions of the evil and fire of Hell with this specific 7/100 numerical *graduatio* are commonplace motifs in insular homiletics.[121] In this regard, Christopher Abram has demonstrated how the text of *De natiuitate domini* in the *NHB* has a formal parallel in an Anglo-Saxon homily edited under the name *Be heofonwarum and be helwarum* (*BHH*).[122] Its text is transmitted in two manuscripts copied at the turn of the twelfth century and employs the very same *graduationes* of the fire and evil residing in Hell.[123] The presence of both motifs within a single Anglo-Saxon text naturally corroborates the idea that the reference to the hundred tongues of iron may already have been included in the original insular homily, whether in Latin or Old English, from which the Norse text is derived. As a consequence, the presence of the Virgilian cliché in the *NHB* does not necessarily imply a direct or comprehensive knowledge of the *VP* in early thirteenth-century Norway. Moreover, it seems clear from the collations below that the Virgilian *graduatio* in the *NHB* cannot possibly have been borrowed from the corresponding passage of *PLe*, which, on the contrary, shares a significantly more similar lexicon and wording with *DLe*:

NHB 34/2–5 (AM 619)	DLe 74/13–16 (AM 681a)	PLe 39a–39b (A)	PLe 39a–39b (B)
Oc þo at hværr maðr hæfði hundrað hofða. ok í hværiu hofði være .c. tugna or iarne. ok þær allar mælte fra uphafe hæimſ þeſſa. alt til veraldar enda. þa mætte þær ægi ſægia allt þat hit illa er í hælviti er.	En huilikar e(da) huersu miklar og hardar pislir er hon sæ þar þoat c tungna uæri þar j hueriu hofdi þa mundi eigi geta up talt *fatt er þat sem hann sagdi os.	Páll postoli spurði eingil hversu margar píslir voru í helvíti. Eingill svarar. Þó at væri hundrað tungna ok væri ortalin þá vinnask þér eigi til at telja allar píslir er í helvíte eru.	[inc B] píslir voru í helvíti. Eingill sagði. Þó at væri hundrað tungna ok væri ortali þá vinnask þær eigi til at telja allar píslir er í helvíte eru.

---

[121] See for instance Wright 1993, 145–48 and 219–21 on the iron tongues and the fire of Hell respectively.

[122] Abram 2004, 33 and Abram 2007, 442–43. The connection was first suggested by Johnson 1993, 414–31.

[123] London, BL, Cotton Faustina A.IX and Cambridge, Corpus Christi College, 302. Both manuscripts were transcribed in south-east England. The text is edited in Teresi 2002, 211–44.

BHH 229	DLe 74/27–28 (W)	VP 39a–b (L12)	VP 39a–b (L12)
Þeah ænig man hæfde .c. heafda and þæra heafda æghwilc hæfde .c. tungan and hi wæron ealle isene and ealle spræcon fram frymðe þyssere worulde oð ende ne mihton hi asecgan þæt yfel þe on helle is.	[E]t quanta vel qualia et quam inaudita ibi viderit tormenta, si centum capita et in uno quoque capite centum linguas haberet, recitare nullo modo posset.	Et interrogavit Paulus angelum, quot pene essent in inferno. Cuis ait angelus: Sunt pene centum quadraginta tria mila. Et si essent centum viri loquentes ab inicio mundi et unusquisque centum linguas ferreas haberet, non possent dinumerare penas inferni.	Et interrogavit Paulus angelum, quot pene essent in inferno. Cuis ait angelus: Sunt pene centum quadraginta tria mila. Et si essent centum viri loquentes ab inicio mundi et unusquisque centum linguas ferreas haberet, non possent dinumerare penas inferni.

Whereas *PLe* and *DLe* employ the verb (*upp*)*telja* 'to count, to enumerate', translating the Latin *enumerare* of the source,[124] the *NHB* has the verb *segja* 'to tell, report' that corresponds exactly with the Old English *asecgan* 'to tell, report'. In turn, the Old English form is in all probability derived from the Latin *narrare*/*enarrare* rather than *enumerare*, as five manuscripts of the *VP* transmitting a text of type C, mostly of English provenance, seem to suggest.[125] Additionally, both *DLe* and *PLe* omit the description of the iron metal of which the tongues are composed, and whereas Paul and Duggall wonder about the precise number of the pains or torments of Hell (*VP* 'quot pene essent in inferno'/*VT* 'quanta vel qualia et quam inaudita ibi viderit tormenta'), the *NHB* and *BHH* speculate on *all* the wickedness of Hell (*BHH* 'þæt yfel þe on helle is'/*NHB* 'þat hit illa er í hælviti er'). The latter uncountable noun, along with the adjective, are in all probability an anticipation of a reading yet to come, 'omnia ista mala', which is typical of the last homiletic ending of the C group (41).

[124] The Latin source text behind *DLe* might have also had the verb *narrare*/ *enarrare* rather than the *recitare* 'recite, declaim' found in W.

[125] *Narrare* is found in Padua, Biblioteca Antoniana, 473, Scaff. XXI, ff. 147v–149r (Pa), A2 group, northern Italy, *c*.1200; Dublin, Trinity College, TDC 519, ff. 95ra–96rb (D^3), C3 group, England, *c*.1450; Oxford, Merton College, Ms 13, ff. 63vb–64vb (O^5), C3 group, Oxford, *c*.1400–50; *enarrare* is found in London, BL, Royal 11.B.III, f. 334va–vb (L^9), C/spec group, England, *c*.1300; Paris, BnF, lat. 5266, ff. 21vb–23va (P^8), C/spec group, unknown provenance, *c*.1200.

Some passages in *PLe* that find no correspondence in the *VP* might, on the other hand, be indebted, at least through mnemonic repetition or distant echoes, to some of the sermons collected in the *NHB* or might have arisen from similar texts circulating in the same monastic environment. Interestingly, the three possible borrowings are all added towards the end of the narrative and inserted into Christ's own speech. There are strikingly similar verbal parallels in Christ's description of his crucifixion with three nails (34c),[126] which echoes a similar formula employed with reference to Christ and the Trinity by the homilist of *In die omnium sanctorum sermo* extant both in the *NHB* and in the *IHM*;[127] in Christ's rebukes to humankind (34d)[128] with the admonitory words of the homilist in the *Sermo necessaria* of the *NHB*;[129] and possibly soon after in Christ's additional remark in which he laments humankind's ingratitude for his mildness (34d/add)[130]—a passage that reminds the reader of his words in the aforementioned *De natiuitate domini sermo* of the *NHB*.[131]

Páls leizla and Icelandic Texts

Tveitane further suggested that two medieval Icelandic texts might owe some of their literary motifs to the text of the *VP*. He points to two passages of *Páls saga postola* II, a composite text written during the second half of the thirteenth century, and *Mikjáls saga*, drawn from a great variety of sources by the priest Bergr Sokkason, fourteenth-century abbot of Munkaþverá († c.1370) (*En norrøn versjon av Visio Pauli* 1964, 22–23). As I shall try to demonstrate below, however, textual evidence does not seem to support his assertions.

[126] A '[E]k var þremr nauglum negldur.' See section on 'Christology' below.
[127] '[Þ]rimr naufnum næmdr í fkilningu. faðer. ok. fonr. ok ande heilagr' (*NHB* 144/5 and *IHB* 18v/16).
[128] A 'En þér létud í móti koma lygi ok lausung dramb ok manndrap ok ágirni ok ǫfund, skrǫkvitni ok munneiða, hórdóm ok lostasemi hlátr ok skelki ofát ok ofdrykkju leti ok líkamsmunuð mikilléti.'
[129] 'Sia við mandrape ok við hordome. við ftuldum. við fcrøcvitnum. við mæin-æiðum. við ráne. við rauhgum dome . . . / . . . við lygi. við laufung . . . / . . . við gauldrum. við gerningum. við mykillæte' (*NHB*, 87/23–30). This affinity was already noted in Tveitane, ed., *En norrøn versjon av Visio Pauli*, 16.
[130] A 'En þér villduð ekki gefa til minna þakka hvorki mat né drykk.'
[131] 'Hvat gerðu þer fyrir mic á veroldo fiðan ec þolda fva mykit fyrir yðr. Ec gaf yðr fol-fkín. ok rægn. ok iarðar blóm. mat ok clæðe. lif ok hæilfu. en þér kunnuð mer ænga þoc' (*NHB*, 34/25–28).

After a paraphrase of 2 Corinthians 11:24–31, a passage describing the dangers and deprivations of Paul's apostleship, the compiler of *Páls saga postola* II continues his commentary following the natural order of Paul's letter. First, he quotes Paul in 2 Corinthians 12:2–6 on his otherworldly experience[132] and subsequently speaks in the first person, briefly introducing a short passage describing Paul's ascension into the third heaven (*Páls saga postola* II 1874, 268/2–27):

> Her er umræða, hvert Pall var þa hafiðr, er hann var uppnuminn til ens þriðia himins, ok skilia þat sva helgir feðr, at honum væri þa synt himinriki, fyr þvi at þat er himinn kallaðr i helgum ritningum, sem Moyses vattar i upphafi sinnar bokar . . . / . . . En þvi er himinriki enn þriði himinn, at þat er yfir þeim tveim, er aðr voru nefndir, ok sa Pall postoli himneska dyrð ok leynda luti eilifrar sælu, þeirar er vera skal eptir domsdag. En þat er hann segir, at hann var leiddr i paradisum, þa glosa þat sva helgir feðr, at honum hafi syndir verit hvilldarstaðir, er rettlatra manna andir skolu hafa til domsdags.

As the compiler of *Páls saga postola* II himself makes clear, this passage is an exegetical treatment of 2 Corinthians 12:2–6, in which the name *tertium caelum* or third heaven is identified with the *emphyrium caelum* or *elldligr himinn* that was made during the first day of Creation, here described along with the first and second heavens.[133] In point of fact, there seems to be no explicit reference to the text of the *VP* itself nor to its Old Norse adaptation. As already mentioned, the Hell Redaction—from which groups A, B and C and ultimately the Norse text are derived—is centred exclusively on Paul's travel to Hell and entirely omits his journey to Paradise. Furthermore, it seems clear that if the author of *Páls saga postola* II had indeed some knowledge of the *VP*, he could have referred to it within his subsequent description

---

[132] 'Veit ek mann fyr xiiii. vetrum hafðan upp til hins þriðia himins ok sia þar leynda luti almattigs guðs; en guð veit, hvart hann var bæði með aund ok likama, eða var aundin ein saman, en þat veit ek eigi, segir postolinn, at sa enn sami maðr með þvi moti, sem aðr var sagt, var leiddr i paradis ok heyrði þar þau orð, er manni er eigi leyft at mæla her i veraulldu. Fyr þessa sauk, segir Pall postoli, mætta ek hellzt dyrkaz, en ecki fyr minar sakir; ok þo at ek giorða, þa mætti mer eigi virða til ovizku, fyr þvi at ek munda sannedi segia, en ek mun þo við vægiaz, at eigi beri sva i moti, at ne einn, sa er mik ser eða min orð heyrir, ætli mik umfram þat, sem hann ser með mer eða heyrir' (*Páls saga postola* II 1874, 267/24–268/1).

[133] Respectively, the *festingarhiminn* or *firmamentum* with the fixed stars, created on the second day of the week, and the *hvilldarstaðr* or the place of rest, in which the souls of the just abide until Doomsday (*Páls saga postola* II 1874, 268/6–269/12). For explanations of the three heavens in *Páls saga postola* II, see especially Collings 1969, 48–50.

of the third location of Hell, the *puteus inferni* or *pyttr helvítis*, thus further achieving a mirror image of the tripartite outlook of heaven and Hell, for which he seems to be aiming in this section of the text.[134] The third Hell is indeed the very location to which Michael accompanies Paul according to the *VP*,[135] yet *Páls saga postola* II describes it only in passing as a place inhabited by the souls of the capital sinners, from which it is impossible to escape.[136] A similar description of the otherworldly levels of heaven and Hell that includes both the *caelum emphyreum* and the *puteus inferni*, though listing five rather than six locations, is given in the near-contemporary theological summula *Rotulus pugillaris*, written by the Dominican Augustine of Dacia († 1282) around 1260.[137]

Tveitane also notes a vision connected to Roland's death, allegedly experienced by Archbishop Turpin of Reims († 800) and described in *Mikjáls saga*, that might be directly indebted to the *VP*.[138] In a short preamble, Bergr Sokkason declares that the source consulted for the following exemplum is Vincent of Beauvais's *Speculum historiale* († 1264)[139] and subsequently goes on to recount how, while Turpin was celebrating mass at the very moment in which Roland and King Marsirium died in battle, he saw the latter's soul being seized from aloft by a group of black devils and taken to the agonies of Hell, whereas Roland's soul

[134] The other two being the *limbus inferni*, from which Abraham was fetched by Christ, and the *hreinsanastaðr* or *purgatorium*, inhabited by the repentant sinners (*Páls saga postola* II 1874, 269/16–270/2); see discussion in Collings 1969, 51.

[135] The *puteus/pyttr* hosting the unbelievers in Christ is mentioned in scenes 28, 28a, 28d.

[136] 'Enn þriði staðr i helviti heitir puteus inferni, þat þyðiz pyttr helvitis, ok fara þangat þeira manna salur, er i haufuðsyndum lataz ok rekningar eru fra guði, ok leysiz engi or þeim stað, sa er þangat kemr' (*Páls saga postola* II 1874, 269/34–270/2).

[137] Within a section on penance, Augustine clarifies: 'Et nota quod quinque sunt loca animarum exutarum usque ad iudicium slicet caelum empyreum, limbus patrum, sinus puerorum non baptizatorum, purgatorium, de quo dictum est, et puteus inferni' (Augustinus de Dacia, *Rotulus pugillaris*, 563/27).

[138] See Tveitane 1963, 106–111 and *En norrøn versjon av Visio Pauli* 1965, 27–28. Subsequently doubts on this attribution have been expressed in Wellendorf 2009, 141–42.

[139] 'Su bok heitir Speculum Historiale, er þat vattar, at virðuligr herra Turpin erkibyskup Reinsborgar var eigi i þeim bardaga, er giorðiz i Runzival . . . / . . . Þvi vattar þat fyrr nefnd bok, at æ sama dag sem orrostan var i Runzival, songh Turpin erkibyskup sælumessu' (*Mikjáls saga*, 692/3–8).

Introduction

was guided into the eternal bliss of heaven by Michael himself (*Mikjáls saga*, 692/10–29):[140]

> Ok er erkibyskupinn stendr i messuembættinu, er hann upptekinn i andar syn ok litr i loptinu, hvar fara haleitir flokkar heilagra hirðsveita með songh ok sætum hlioðum, meðr birti ok bloma miklum, sva at byskupinum gefr æ at lita ok heyra, þar til at su himneska ferð firriz sva miogh iarðrikit, at honum hverfr at syn upp i loptið. Hann hugleiðir með ser, hvat þesse syn mun hafa at þyða, ok litlu siðarr ser hann ferd aðra miog olika; i þessarri ferd eru svartir dioflar hardleitir ok helvitlegir asyndum, þeir eru margir saman ok hafa nockut meðferdar, þat er þeir þysia at ollum megum sem dioflar at agni dauðans. Turpin erkibyskup verpr ordum æ þa ok segir sva: 'H(v)at dragi þer eða starfit.' Þeir svara: 'Ver drogum felagha varn Marsirium konung til eilifðar kvalar i helvitis herað, en Mikhael styrir þeiri ferð, er leidir luðrþeytara yðvarn upp i himnana.' Af þessari birting vissi erkibyskup tiðendi ok sagði konunginum, hvat guð hafði synt honum. Ok litlu siðar kom Balldvini broder Rollanz æ mæddum vapnhesti váttandi somu tiðendi, sem aðr voru greind, hvaðan ver munum fra venda, þviat nu er vitni borit, at Mikael fylgir voldum monnum til eilifra fagnada.

The closest possible source proposed by Tveitane for this passage is an Early Middle High German poem, written in rhymed couplets and extant in *codex unicus* in the thirteenth-century Vienna, Österreichische Nationalbibliothek, Ser. Nova 388, f. 2r–v, a bifolium dated to around 1300, which describes the souls of a sinner and a just man sharing fates similar to those of Roland and King Marsirium.[141] In this context, however, the good soul is allegorically described as being chosen by a certain unnamed angel as his own wife and accompanied to heaven where they shall reside together (*Deutsche Sprach-Denkmale* 1846, 112/6–20):

> Der tivel in lat die fele. Zv dem grabe niht mere. Er wuret fi wider in die not. folich ift der funder tot . . . / . . . Der guten vñ der rechten. In diner befschowede trechtin . . . / . . . Der engel durch fin gvote Der fi fschol behvten. So ift der engil fo der man Der ime eine vil liebe gemalen gwan. Er famenit fich wil witen. Durch willen finer brute. Mit vrunden ioch mit magen. Er in lat fich ez niht betragen. Mit menigen kumet er wur daz huf. Die vrowen ladit er dar vz. Er halfet vñ cuffet fin trout. Dan wuret er die brut.

While one might notice a distant resemblance between the two texts, the association of the Vienna bifolium with the text of the *VP* is based on an old misconception. As Volker Mertens has shown, the Early Middle High German verses, subsequently named *Von der Zukunft nach dem*

---

[140] On this passage, see especially Foote 1959, 23–24.
[141] The text is edited in *Deutsche Sprach-Denkmale* 1846, 109/1–112/24.

Tode, draw on a variety of twelfth-century sources, including Honorius Augustodunensis's († 1154) *Elucidarium* and various homilies, in which the same *topos* of an evil soul captured by the devil is found. Confusion in previous scholarship has arisen because the High German verses draw on the same ancient body–soul *topos*, which enjoyed enormous popularity throughout the Middle Ages and on which numerous Latin and vernacular texts are based.[142] However, the most important literary motif, the allegorical description of the soul as an angel's bride, shared by the *VP* (32a),[143] *Von der Zukunft nach dem Tode* and the *Elucidarium*, is completely absent in *Mikjáls saga*. Moreover, and perhaps most importantly, there is no deliverance of the souls to heaven on Michael's part either in the Hell Redaction of the *VP* or *PLe*, in which the archangel's role, rather than that of a psychopomp, is that of intercessor to grant the souls respite on Sundays.

It seems clear that Bergr Sokkason might have taken this exemplum from any one of a variety of other sources that describe the travel of a good soul to Paradise, and the possibility cannot be excluded that the version of *Speculum historiale* he was consulting already included this passage in the form of an interpolation or perhaps as a marginal gloss. Whatever the case may be, the text of the *VP* or *PLe* cannot be credited as the immediate or the ultimate source for this passage in *Mikjáls saga*.

Christology

After Paul and Michael deliver their intercessional prayer, the voice of Christ the Lord is heard from heaven above (34b).[144] In the Latin text he first asks the sinners, in a reproachful tone, the reason behind their request for a respite from the anguish and misery of Hell if they have wilfully conducted an earthly life of sin and perdition (34b), then proceeds in both texts to list the offences he suffered during his crucifixion (34c; 34d/add).

> Ek var krossfestr fyrir yðrar sakir ok ek var þremr nǫglum negldr. Mér var gefit eitr at drekka ok ek þoldi háðuligar hrakningar ok ⟨varð⟩ við verði seldr. Síðan þoldi ek drap ok dauða fyrir yðr at þér skylduð vera með mér í eilífum fagnadi . . . / . . . Ek léða yðr allt þat er þér þurftuð at hafa en þér villduð ekki

---

[142] On the subject see especially Mertens 1975, 77–92. For an overview of the body–soul literature of the Middle Ages, see the collection of essays in Boitani Torti 1999.

[143] L[12] 'O beata anima, o felicissima sponsa, o beata in Christo, letare, quia fecisti hodie voluntatem Dei tui!' It is only alluded to in *PLe*: 'Gleðsk þú hin helga því at þú gørðir þíns Dróttins vilja ok alldri skáltu þína samvist við hana skilja.'

[144] 'Ok þa svarar dróttinlig rǫdd svá mælandi.'

gefa til minna þakka hvorki mat né drykk. Óverðugr er sá at þiggja miskunnina seigir bókin er ǫngva vill ǫdrum veita.

While *PLe* essentially retains the most salient elements of Christ's rebuke, it also adds some highly significant idiosyncrasies that reflect contemporary christological precepts and provide invaluable insights into the type of impression the Norse compiler wished to imprint on the vernacular text. For example, Christ testifies to having been nailed to the cross with three nails ('ek var þremr nǫglum negldr') rather than with four; a reading that seems to be unique in the Old Norse corpus. The only other instance of specification of the precise number of nails employed in the Crucifixion is found in the *Purificatio sanctae Mariae* sermon of the *IHB* for the 2nd February Candlemas festivity. Here four nails are counted; two of them fastened his hands and two his feet, which inflicted four of the holy wounds in addition to the fifth in his side where he was pierced by Longinus with his lance (*IHB* 39r/20–24):

> Drótten vár ſat gyþingom morg méinmǽle oc ſáran bardaga. ſtórlega píning. eſ han lét ſic negla a cros fiórom nǫglom tueim í hendr. oþrom tueim í føtr. til hialpar os ſkírþom monom. han vaſ ſǽrþr a croſſe eno fimta ſáre meþ ſpióte einſ ríþera. þes eſ longinuſ heiter.[145]

It is perhaps significant that in the corresponding text of the *NHB* no mention is made of the four nails.[146] In a second example, within the *In inventione sanctae crucis* sermon, the *NHB* seems again to avoid mentioning the precise number of nails employed in the Crucifixion and simply gives an allegorical explanation of the different parts of the cross: the arms symbolise love towards God and men, whereas the lower part of the cross, onto which the two feet are nailed, represents the steadfastness of the good deeds of humanity during the worldly life.[147] No mention is made of the number of nails in AM 234 fol. (*c*.1340), transmitting *Maríu saga* II, in which the compiler reminds the reader that the blood of Christ was shed five times in all: during his circumcision (Luke 2:21), when his sweat turned into blood in the Garden of Gethsemane (Luke 22:44), when he was scourged

---

[145] Bede's *Homilia* 18 *In purificatione beatae Mariae* and Ambrosius Autpertus's *Sermo in purificatione sanctae Mariae* have been identified as possible sources of the homily. The texts are edited in *CCSL* 122, 128–33 and *PL* 89, 1291–1304 respectively. See discussion in McDougall 1983, 381 n. 40.

[146] The homily is edited in *NHB* 66/21–69/22.

[147] 'En armar croſſ-ens merkia tvinna æſt við guð ok menn. Sa lutr croſſenſ er hæſtr er. merkir en guðſ æſt. en armarnir nǫngſ ælſco bǽðe við víni ok óvini. Føtr ero ender licams. þvi iartæinir ſa lutr croſſ-enſ er føtr hans vǽro á negldir ſtaðfeſte goðra verka alt til enda lífs' (*NHB* 104/14–18).

(Matthew 27:26), when he was crucified and his feet were nailed on the cross (Matthew 27:35), and when his side was pierced (John 19:34).[148] In medieval Latin literature, the first occurrence of a three-nail Crucifixion is found in *Sermo* 166 (*in uigilia paschatis*) by William of Auvergne († 1249), theologian and bishop of Paris from 1228, who compares the three nails to monastic observance, which comprises the vows of poverty, chastity and obedience.[149] Around 1236, in the second book of his *De altera vita*, the first treatise against heretics in medieval Spain, Lucas de Tuy († 1249) takes a stern tone when mentioning the twelfth-century Albigensian heresy, which contemplated three rather than four nails and asserted that the fifth holy wound was on Christ's left rather than on his right side.[150] Towards the end of the thirteenth century in his *Rationale divinorum officiorum*, a treatise on the symbolic elements of churches and church ornaments, Guillaume Durand († 1296) attests the existence of both traditions, and asserts that while the four nails symbolise the four virtues of justice, fortitude, moderation and prudence, the three nails are allegories of the Passion in the body, in the mind and in the heart.[151]

[148] 'Fyrst er hann var skirðr vmskvrðar skirnn; ok vm nottina, aðr at hann væri handtekinn, þaa svettiz hann bloði aa bæn sinni; hit þriðia sinn, þaa er hann var bvndinn við stolpann ok barðr; fiorða sinn, þaa er hann var krossfestr ok fætr vorv neglldir a krossinn; hit fimta sinn, þaa er Longinvs lagði spioti i siðv honvm, ok rann a sarinv bloð ok vatnn' (*Maríu saga*, 386/30–387/6). The same section is also found in the encyclopaedic material of AM 731 4to (*c*.1600–50) under the rubric *Af gráti Christi* (*Alfræði íslenzk* III, 1918, 8/11–19).

[149] 'Mortui debent esse omnes mundo et peccatis, ita quod nulla uita quantum ad hoc in eis appareat, uel sic mortui cum Christo, id est simili morte in cruce, scilicet crucifixi tribus clauis, uoto paupertatis, castitatis et obedientie. Crux ipsa obseruancia claustralis est' (Guillelmus Alvernus, *Sermo* 166 (*in uigilia paschatis*) 2001, 132/9–13).

[150] 'Fecerunt tunc temporis supradicti haeretici crucem cum tribus brachiis tantum, in qua erat imago uno pede super alio, tribus clauis eidem cruci affixa, quae brachio eminentiori carebat . . . / . . . Similitudo autem crucis illius, quam tribus clauis et tribus brachiis non sine scandalo mutarunt animarum, in quibusdam ecclesiis pietatis studio adoratur . . . / . . . Sufficit ad salutem Christum credere crucifixum et pro indifferenti habere in cruce illum quatuor uel trium brachiorum fuisse positum, quatuor uel tribus clauis confixum et dextrum uel sinistrum latus eius lancea uulneratum' (Lucas Tudensis, *De altera uita* 2009, 121/155; 122/1; 132/152).

[151] 'Quatuor clavi sunt quatuor principales virtutes, scilicet justitia, fortitudo, temperantia, et prudentia . . . / . . . Alii tamen dicunt quod Christus tribus duntaxat fuit clavis affixus, significantibus tres cruciatus, quos in Cruce sustinuit, videlicet passionem in corpore, passionem in mente, et passionem in corde' (Durandus, *Rationale divinorum officiorum* 1859, 537/1–2; 14–16).

Subsequently, around 1300, Ramón Llull († 1316) also describes Christ crucified with three nails in his *Liber de homine*.[152] Besides these sporadic occurrences in thirteenth-century sources, the work that influenced the later decision to portray Christ with three nails was the Pseudo-Bonaventure's *Meditationes vitae Christi*, of debated authorship, but certainly connected to the Franciscan circle since it is addressed to a Poor Claire, written in northern Italy during the middle of the fourteenth century. The author describes a violent crucifixion in which Christ suffers greatly, affixed so tightly to the three nails of the cross that he can move neither his body nor his head and bears unbearable agonies.[153]

The visual representation of the three nails of the Passion, which subsequently prevailed throughout the later Middle Ages, seems to have originated in the first half of the thirteenth century as a stylistic development of the older crucifixes. Two feet fastened to the cross with one nail, a position that required bent legs and a collapsed body, came to replace the older, more composed Christ suspended with parallel feet and four nails. The new excruciating posture of the crucifix conferred an impression of great sorrow and moved devotees all the more with pity and compassion towards the sacrificed Christ.[154] Significantly, along with the three nails, in the same decades the crown of thorns described in the Gospels (Matthew 27:29; Mark 15:17; John 19:2; John 19:5) was introduced and replaced the old diadem, a symbol of royalty worn by the victorious King of kings and sovereign ruler depicted in the Apocalypse (Revelation 19:12).[155] In Norway in particular, three-nail crucifixes start making their appearance along with the crown of thorns in the second half

---

[152] 'Domine Iesu Christe, tu cum tribus clauis fortissimis clauatus fuisti et in terram euersus, ut crux supra te foret, in qua claui fuerunt replicati, ut plus fores derisus et tormentatus' (Raimundus Lullus, *Liber de homine*, 281/316).

[153] 'Ecce crucifixus est Dominus Iesus, et sic in cruce extensus quod dinumerari omnia ossa eius possunt, sicut per Prophetam ipse conqueritur. Fluunt undique sacratissimi sanguinis riuuli ex illis magnis scissuris. Sic que coangustatus est quod se mouere non potest nisi in capite. Illi tres claui sustinent tocius corporis eius pondus; dolores acerbissimos tolerat et ultra quam dici uel cogitari possit affligitur' (Iohannes de Caulibus, *Meditaciones vitae Christi* 1977, 53–57).

[154] On three-nail crucifixes, see especially Wirth 1958, 524–25 and Wirth 1953.

[155] In 1238 Louis IX († 1270) purchased the Crown of Thorns from the Emperor of Constantinople Baldwin II Porphyrogenitus († 1273) and placed it in the royal chapel (Sainte-Chapelle) of the Île de la Cité. The relic soon became widely venerated in Paris and throughout western Europe and the cult greatly influenced the visual arts. On the historical acquisition of the relic, see for instance Nicol 1998, repr. 1999, 169–70.

of the thirteenth century in crucifixes ascribed to the English craftsmen of the time.[156] Along with the crown of thorns, the holy lance, the holy sponge and other instruments of the Passion, the three nails began to be included among the *arma Christi* and their veneration became commonplace in late-medieval popular piety. It is very likely that the Norse compiler had one of these representations in mind when he listed Christ's abuses prior to the Crucifixion.[157] One such depiction is extant in AM 683 d 4to, a fragment leaf of Norwegian provenance, dated *c*.1385–99, which preserves a moving illumination of the Man of Sorrow, with hands bound together before his chest and a cruciform halo. Six instruments of the Passion are portrayed: the holy grail, which collects the blood running from his wounds, the crown of thorns, a three-tongued scourge, a reed sceptre, a hammer and the three nails.[158] This image of the *Vir dolorum*, which became particularly popular

---

[156] It should be noted that while the Norwegian Balke, Fåberg, Tretten, Kjose, Hedal, Heggen, Trondheim, Bergen, Solum, Rødenes, Hølandet, Elverum, Hamre, the Swedish Mofalla, Tossene, Rännelanda, and the Danish Bellinge crucifixes from the second half of the thirteenth century all depict a crown of thorns and three nails, on the Norwegian Fresvik and Østsinni crucifixes, dating from the first half of the same century, Christ is crucified with three nails but wears a royal crown and thus seem to constitute an intermediate stage of the iconography. See the excellent survey by Andersson 1949, 130–31; 142–45; 185–99; 244–47; 259–63.

[157] During proofreading, I discovered that f. 14v of AM 673 a III 4to, better known as *Íslenska teiknibókin*, the *Icelandic Model-book*, preserves a faded depiction of John the Evangelist and Mary attending the crucified Christ framed by twenty-two compartments containing the *arma Christi* with the corresponding Latin *titula*: 'lanterna' (the lantern); 'calix' (the Holy Grail); 'veronica' (the veil of Veronica); 'pellicanus' (the pelican); 'vrceus' (the pitcher); 'tunica' (the tunic); 'corona spinea' (the crown of thorns); 'malleus fustes' (the hammer, the clubs); 'spongea' (the sponge); 'claui' (the nails); 'cutellus' (the knife of the circumcision); 'forceps' (the tongs); 'monumentum' (the tomb); 'velum templi' (the veil of the temple); 'serpens' (the serpent), 'triginta argintei' (the thirty slices of sliver); 'flagella' (the scourges); 'lancea' (the lance); 'gladij' (the swords); 'sckala' (the ladder), 'cholumpna corda' (the pillar), 'arundines' (the reeds). The holy nails, which occupy the second compartment from the bottom right side of the folio, are three in number. The depiction was executed by the so-called C-Artist around 1450–75 in a yet unidentified scriptorium of Northern Iceland. A brief description and reproduction of f. 14v are available in Guðbjörg Kristjánsdóttir 2013, 134–35.

[158] The fragment was used as a flyleaf and glued together with AM 683 c 4to, a single Norwegian leaf transmitting a *Jólaskrá*. For the date and provenance of the manuscript, I rely exclusively on http://handrit.is/is/manuscript/view/da/AM04-

in northern Europe after 1350, is often included in the *Book of Hours*, where it precedes either the Hours of the Holy Cross or the Penitential Psalms.[159] Indeed, the Latin text that precedes the illumination is the concluding section of the *Deus qui pro redemptione mundi* prayer to the crucifix, which is otherwise known under several other titles.[160] The text relates how Christ was fully aware and willing to be betrayed by Judas, bound in fetters, sacrificed like an innocent lamb, insulted and spat upon, crowned with thorns, wounded with a spear, pierced with nails, forced to drink vinegar and gall, and to die for humanity.

⟨Deus qui pro redemptione mundi voluisti nasci circumcidi a iudeis reprobari a iuda traditore osculo tradi vinculis alligari sicut agnus innocens ad victimam duci atque conspectibus anne caiphe pilato et herodi indecenter offerri a falsis testibus accusari flagellis et opprobriis vexari sputis conspui spinis coronari colaphis cedi arundine percuti facie velari vestibus exui cruci clavis affigi in cruce levari inter latrones d)eputari felle et aceto potari et lancea vulnerari. Tu domine per has sanctissimas passiones tuas quas ego indignissimus peccator recolo et per sanctam crucem tuam libera me de penis inferni et perducere digneris quo perduxisti tecum latronem crucifixum et confitens tecum ad deo patre et filio et spiritu sancto vivis et regnas in secula.[161]

In the right margin, a later text in Old Danish reports the legend of the *Mass of St Gregory*, according to which Gregory had a vision of the suffering Christ in the Church of Santa Croce in Gerusalemme in Rome, who appeared to him above the altar with the instruments of the Passion, displaying his holy wounds.[162]

0683-d, accessed on 2 February 2017. The *ONP* does not list the manuscript and Kålund gives only a summary description (Kålund 1889–94, II 99).

[159] See Kamerick 2002, 169 and Jacoby 2005, 604.

[160] See Leroquais 1927, 45. A variant text of the prayer is edited as *oratio* 2315 in *Corpus orationum*, III, D pars altera, *Orationes 1708–2389*, 1993, 277. See also Kamerick 2002, 169.

[161] The lost section has been integrated from *oratio* 25 in *Enchiridion indulgentiarum*: *preces et pia opera* 1952, 131–25/–132/7.

[162] 'Enn tiid sanctus gregorius pawe sang messo j eno kirkio j Rom som kalles porta crucis widhrd eth altarem som kalles iherusalem oc hann hadhe wigt gudz likame j syntis hanom war herre ihesus christus j blodugs man liknilse oc thii efter messone leth han giør[e] eth swodant bel[et] oc gaff allum them som retscriptad[e] ære [o]c anger fore s[inæ] synder haffwe hwart sinne [the] meth kneffal læse v pater [noster] oc v aue maria fore tolikæ bilæte xiiiim aar afflat effter hanom ga[w]e xii [p]awe hwar there vi aar afflat sidhen gawe [x]xx p[aw]e hwar there ii dagh[a] afflat æff[ter them] gawe xl biscope hwar [there] xl dagha aflat sum offuer.' I have been unable to decipher the last two lines. On the formation of the legend, see for instance Meier 2006.

Fig. 1. Arnamagnæan Collection, AM 683 d 4to, f. 1r (*c.* 1385–99). Photograph by permission of the Arnamagnæan Institute, Copenhagen. Photograph: Suzanne Reitz.

The Christ in scenes 34c and 34d/add in *PLe* should be identified with the aforementioned *Vir dolorum* of the later Middle Ages, and certainly not with the older *Christus victor*, which is most commonly found in the literature and visual arts of the twelfth century.[163] This correlation is even more evident if the following quotation from *PLe* is examined in more detail. After Christ's lamentations towards the sinners, the Norse compiler adds that a specific book, referred to in its definite form as 'the book', instructs Christians to be merciful, since 'the book says' ('seigir bókin') that whoever is unmerciful towards others will in turn not be granted mercy ('Óverðugr er sá at þiggja miskunnina er ǫngva vill ǫðrum veita'). The precise source of this passage has not yet been identified. Jonas Wellendorf has noted that the practice of referring to a specific 'book' or 'books' in the Middle Ages did not necessarily imply that the underlying Latin source included that reference, and has turned to examples of Anglo-Saxon homilists who often referred to 'books' that were not mentioned in the underlying Latin texts they were consulting.[164] He has further rightly maintained that although the sentence finds a thematic counterpart in the Sermon on the Mount (Matthew 6:15),[165] it should not be considered a direct citation from the Scriptures (Wellendorf 2009, 138). There is, however, reasonable evidence to suggest that the Norse scribe is indeed referring to a specific text and that 'the book' is in the definite form since here it means the actual manuscript from which he was copying.

Within the first collection of *Ǽfintýr* translated from Middle English in AM 624 4to, exemplum 29, rubricated as *af einum rikum manni* (37v–38v), relates the story of a profane swearer, a liar and blasphemer, to whom the Virgin Mary appeared in the form of a beautiful woman with a mangled

---

[163] The latter victorious Christ is suitably invoked in *Niðrstigningar saga*, which departs from the original *Gospel of Nicodemus* in quoting Revelation 19:11–17 nearly verbatim, and portraying a warrior-king bright as the sun ready to harrow Hell. He is said to be clothed in royal vestments, wearing a kingly crown, riding a white horse and leading a great army of angels towards the destruction of Hell. On this interpolation see most recently Bullitta forthcoming. On the last interpolation of the text, which describes Christ's defeat of Satan through the hidden divinity of the Cross, see most recently Bullitta 2014, 129–54.

[164] See Wellendorf 2009, 138–39 and references there.

[165] 'But if you will not forgive men, neither will your Father forgive your offences' ('si autem non dimiseritis hominibus nec Pater vester dimittet peccata vestra'). The citation might ultimately also echo the admonishing aphorism concerning judgment of James 2:13: 'For judgment without mercy to him that hath not done mercy. And mercy exalteth itself above judgment' ('iudicium enim sine misericordia illi qui non fecit misericordiam superexultat autem misericordia iudicio.')

child on her lap.[166] The child had a broken head, arms and legs, and his eyes had been drawn out of his body. Mary asks the swearer what would the man who inflicted such horrible injuries on her child deserve and he answers that the abuser should be accorded all the evil one can bear. Mary replies that he should account for having dismembered her child with his great oaths and life of sins but also adds that regardless of his cruelty, she has prayed for Christ to come before him so that the man could ask him for mercy. Upon Christ's appearance, the swearer admits that he feels unworthy to be heard and Christ replies that while he is 'unworthy' ('óverðugr') to be heard for his sins and has forsaken him [i.e. Christ] through sinning, Christ has never forsaken the swearer and has instead proved his immense love by suffering the great abuses of the Passion for him. The swearer replies that he will not ask for mercy even though Christ might want to save him, since his righteousness will not permit it ('hann segir nei til þo þin miskunn uili þiggia mig þa segir þin rettuisi nei'). Nevertheless, Christ insists a second time that he should ask for mercy. Subsequently, when the swearer refuses again, Christ puts a hand into his pierced side, takes out blood, throws it into the sinner's face and says: 'This blood shall bear witness against you at Doomsday that I have offered you mercy' (*Æf* 87/44–53; 88/60–63):

> [Þ]ui so segir uorr herra at eg se ouerdugr at uera heyrdr segir hann. ef þu ert ouerdugr segir uorr herra at uera heyrdr fyrir þinar syndir og hefir fyrir lated mig enn alldri þui helldr fyrir læt eg þig. þui eg hefi þig so dyrt keypt med minni pinu er eg þolldi fyrir þig. og þar fyrir beidztu miskunnar. og þu skallt hafa miskunn. hann segir nei til þo þin miskunn uili þig(g)ia mig þa s(egir) þin rettuisi nei. Huersu skyllda eg hafa miskunn þar sem eg hefi alla mina daga lifat j syndum . . . / . . . og þa segir at worr herra liet sina hond j sitt sidusar ok tok vt sitt blod og kastar framan j anndlitid æ honum so segiandi. þetta blod berr uitni æ moti þier æ doms degi at eg byd þier miskunn.

Thereafter Christ and Mary ascend into heaven, while the profane swearer is taken to the devil to dwell in the everlasting wretchedness of Hell.

It is clear that the author of *PLe* alludes to this exemplum of the *Gesta Romanorum* at the most appropriate point within the original Latin text, that is after Christ's rebuke to the sinners (34c; 34d). By including this quotation as the very last words of Christ (34d/add), he is consciously adding a final admonition to the sinners, and by extension a warning to

---

[166] The exemplum is edited in *Æf* 84/1–88/66 with the corresponding Middle English text, rubricated as *Of the Death-Bed of a Profane Swearer*. In the following discussion, I refer to the sinner as 'the profane swearer' as he is called in the original Middle English text, rather than with the Icelandic rubric 'a rich man'.

the audience to repent and beg for mercy before it is too late. It is implied that Christ would grant mercy to anyone who asks for it, unless like the profane swearer they persevere in sinning during their lives, thus extending the atrocities of the Passion, since Christ, like the mangled Child, pays daily for the sins of humankind. In this respect, the sinners of *PLe* meet a slightly more fortunate fate than that of the profane swearer: after they have begged for mercy through Paul and Michael's intercessional prayers, in the following scene (34g) God grants them a Sunday respite, sparing them from the horrible tortures of Hell one day every week until Doomsday.

A second reference to 'the book', the material manuscript consulted and copied by the Norse compiler, is found in the vernacular text just after the Sunday respite has been granted to the sinners (37). The complier notes again that 'at this point [the] book says' ('Nú mælir svá bókin') that God pronounced these words: 'Sá er heldr vel hina helga dróttinsdag ok hinn helga píslardag Vors Herra Ihesu Christi ok gengr réttiliga til skrifta hann skal réttliga með Guði vera utan enda.'[167] There is an exact counterpart to this sentence in the Latin *VP*, although there, rather than being pronounced by God, these are the words of the omniscient narrator since they refer to God in the third person and can be attributed to neither Paul nor Michael: 'Et qui custodierunt hunc sanctum diem habuerunt partem cum angelis Dei et vitam sempiternam.'[168] As well as the observance of Sunday as the day of the Lord, the Norse compiler also notes Easter Sunday ('hinn helga píslardag') along with the practice of a good confession ('ok gengr réttiliga til skrifta'), which requires the intention to ask for mercy for and acknowledgement of one's sins. This specification further confirms the prominence given in the vernacular text to the internalisation of Christ's suffering and the contemplation of the Passion for the redemption of sins.

Provenance

This survey of the Latin and vernacular material consulted for the composition of *PLe* has revealed that its text cannot be regarded as the scholarly product of twelfth-century Norway, as Tveitane suggested in his first edition of the text (*En norrøn versjon av Visio Pauli* 1965, 20). Conversely, combined internal and external evidence indicate unambiguously that the text of *PLe* is nearly contemporary to the two late fifteenth-century Icelandic codices transmitting it: AM 624 4to and AM 681 c 4to.

---

[167] 'The one who holds well the holy day of the Lord and the holy day of the Passion of Christ and justly confesses oneself, he shall justly be with God without end.'

[168] 'And those who kept this day holy, have had part with the angels of God and eternal life.'

First, the numerous agreements of the Norse text with L^{12}, a theological miscellany written in the West Midlands around 1400, demonstrate that the lost Latin source text accessed by the Norse compiler was indeed one of the immediate ancestors of L^{12}, in all probability a codex that was in circulation in the same region in the late fourteenth century. Second, amongst his subsidiary amplifications, the compiler seems to make explicit reference to several 'sins of the tongue', offences that had not been classified as capital vices before the middle of the thirteenth century when a whole chapter in William Peraldus's *Summa de vitiis et virtutibus*, the standard handbook for confessors that had become extremely popular in the late Middle Ages, was dedicated to them. Third, the vernacular text expressly refers to heretics burnt at the stake, a capital punishment that became legal only in the late Middle Ages, towards the end of the thirteenth century in France and in the first years of the fifteenth in England.

It appears that the redactor of *PLe* also made abundant use of vernacular sources. He was certainly acquainted with at least two sermons of the *NHB*, *De nativitate domini* and *In die omnium sanctorum*, which are echoed in the additional passages that report Christ's poignant speech to the sinners. The former is evoked within the list of sins committed by humanity and the latter by the expression 'þremr nǫglum negldr' in his description of the Crucifixion. That the compiler of *DLe* had knowledge of the *NHB*—and not the other way around, as Tveitane believed—is further confirmed by the fact that Tveitane's most decisive argument for the latter dependence rested exclusively on the employment of the Virgilian cliché for the hundred tongues of iron in *De nativitate domini* and *PLe*. As Abram has recently demonstrated, however, *De nativitate domini* is, ultimately or directly, indebted to the Anglo-Saxon *BHH* homily, with which it shares numerous details, including similar wording and indeed the use of the Virgilian cliché (Abram 2004, 442–43). Also very unlikely is the dependence, again suggested by Tveitane, of sections of *Páls saga postola* II and *Mikjáls saga* on the texts of either *PLe* or *VP* (*En norrøn versjon av Visio Pauli* 1965, 21–23). As a matter of fact, the two passages he refers to are more likely derived from disparate texts that treat similar eschatological themes and allegorical *topoi* and it is not necessary to postulate a direct borrowing from either text. Such evidence naturally corroborates the supposition that neither *PLe* nor *VP* was circulated in thirteenth- and fourteenth-century Iceland, and that Icelanders of that time had only a cursory knowledge of them, if any.

The christological conceit underlying *PLe* also seems to speak for a late-medieval composition. The crucified Christ was not portrayed with three nails until the second half of the thirteenth century and the three nails came to be repeatedly described and portrayed among the other instruments of the Passion in representations of the Man of Sorrow that are typical of the late Middle Ages. Moreover, allusions to *DLe* and to exemplum 29 of the first collection of *Æf*—which relates to a scarified Christ suffering for the cruel sins of humanity and yet still willing to grant mercy to it—reveal that the text of *PLe* could not possibly have been composed before these two texts were available in the same scriptorium. The first collection of *Æf* in AM 624 4to is believed to have been translated from Middle English at Hólar during the episcopacy of the English Bishop Jón Vilhjálmsson Craxton († 1440) by Jón Egilsson, who was well versed in the English language and served the bishopric as *notarius publicus* between 1429 and 1434.[169] Consequently, these years could be taken as a reasonable *post quem* date for the composition of *PLe* in the form we know it today. It has also been noted that the three manuscripts that transmit the Middle English version of the *Gesta Romanorum* that best represent the Icelandic *Æf* were all written in dialects of the West Midlands,[170] and it is perhaps not a simple coincidence that L^{12}, the closest possible Latin text to *PLe*, was also copied in the West Midlands, only two decades before the arrival in Iceland of Bishop Jón Vilhjálmsson Craxton from England in 1426.[171]

While its acquisition from England puts it in the diocese of Hólar during the second decade of the fifteenth century, its translation could be placed sometime later in the same diocese. As a matter of fact, there are indications that the compiler of *PLe* may have been working at Hólar or in the vicinity in the second half of the fifteenth century, during the regency of the Norwegian Bishop Ólafr Rögnvaldsson († 1495), who held the northern diocese in the years 1450–95. Indeed, the above-mentioned formula *blífa ok vera*, in the infinitive form, is first found in the *Andsvar Norðlendinga um presta og kirkna skyldur*, a document written in 1482 and addressed to Bishop Ólafr Rögnvaldsson (*DI*, VI 462/9–10), and the compound adjective *forstǫðulauss* is first recorded in a *tylftardómr* from Saurbær, about 50 km from Hólar, dated 24 May 1486 (*DI*, VI 570/1).

In the second half of the fifteenth century, Ólafr was undoubtedly the most influential bishop in Iceland and boasted a prestige that greatly

---

[169] See discussion in *Æf*, xciv–xcix and *The Story of Jonatas in Iceland* 1997, xciv.

[170] London, BL, Additional 9066, Cambridge, University Library, Kk.i.6 and Harley 7333. See discussion in *The Story of Jonatas in Iceland* 1997, xciv n. 56.

[171] On Jón Vilhjálmsson Craxton, see especially Björn Þorsteinsson 1970, 144–47.

overshadowed that of his contemporaries at Skálholt. Nephew of his predecessor at Hólar Gottskálk Keniksson and grandson of the Norwegian knight Kenik Gottskálkson, he had strong connections to the archbishopric at Nidaros. He was granted the privilege of sitting on the Norwegian Council of the Realm (*Riksrådet*) and in 1459, the same year as he was elected bishop, he was appointed *sýslumaðr* of the Hegranesþing by Christian I of Denmark († 1481), then King of Norway and Denmark. After his election, Ólafr imposed severe punishments on transgressors against the law and promoted a firm policy of reformation and reorganisation of the diocesan economic system.[172] A great dispute, testified to by the above-mentioned *Andsvar Norðlendinga*, arose in 1482 between Ólafr and the northerners, who were unwilling to finance further the travel costs of the bishop and his retinue and, in general, were tired of bolstering Cathedral funds at the expense of their own parish churches (*DI*, VI 458/9–468/13). Among the lay people Ólafr's arch-enemy was Hrafn Brandsson the Old († 1483), chieftain and *lögmaðr* in the north and the west, who in 1481 was involved in the so-called *Hvassafellsmál* in which Bjarni Ólason, a farmer at Hvassafell, was accused of incest with his daughter Randíðr, who then sought protection from Hrafn (*DI*, VI 377/1–379/2). Hrafn was excommunicated by Bishop Ólafr for offering Randíðr protection and died before recanting and repenting of his sins, thus meeting all possible preconditions for an afterlife of eternal damnation.

It is highly likely that the translation of *PLe* was undertaken at Hólar during this period of turmoil and discontent between the Church, represented by Bishop Ólafr, and the irate northerners. This might explain some additional references in the text that are either absent or highly elusive in the Latin texts of the *VP*: women who defiled themselves under their male relatives (20c); excommunicated men who did not wish to repent and be reconciled with God (28g/add); sinners who made money in an evil manner and pillaged churches (14d/bis), perhaps by refusing to pay tithes to the Cathedral; or even an allusion to the discontent among the northerners who, dissatisfied with the recent administration of their diocese, were disruptive at church while the bishop and his priests sang mass (14a). Moreover, the reading of the Latin text describing the soul of a condemned bishop (26a) remains unmentioned in the Norse text.

Ólafr himself might have requested a translation of the *VP*, after his return from Norway in the winter 1482–83, from Latin manuscript material

---

[172] On Ólafr Rögnvaldsson see especially Líndal 1974, 126–34.

of English provenance that had been deposited at the Hólar scriptorium during the episcopacy of Jón Vilhjálmsson Craxton.[173] The hand of a Norwegian scribe working within the bishop's retinue might indeed explain the peculiar choice of legal vocabulary of ultimate Norwegian provenance that is so typical of *PLe*. The Latin text of the *VP* was in all probability translated and associated with the collection of the Icelandic *Æf*, which was already available at the scriptorium. The same homiletic procedure found in the moralised exempla of the *Gesta Romanorum* was followed for the compilation of other texts that were non-homiletic in origin, among them *PLe*. Hence in 'the book', a fine vernacular miscellany that is twice referred to in *PLe*, one of the immediate ancestors of AM 624 4to, was prepared for the confessors of the diocese to read at communal gatherings perhaps with the intention of preventing the northerners from sinning by showing them all the atrocities that await the souls of unrepentant sinners in Hell for specific trangressions. This very codex might reasonably have been acquired by Jón Þorvaldsson († 1514) at Hólar between 1495 and 1498—that is just after the death of Ólafr Rögnvaldsson—while he was serving there as *officialis* and then taken by him to the monastery of Þingeyrar, where he became abbot and where AM 624 4to was copied.

Edition and Translation

The text of *PLe* transmitted in Reykjavík, Stofnun Árna Magnússonar í íslenskum fræðum, AM 624 4to, ff. 147r–149r (A), here presented in a normalised form, has been divided into the same variants, with corresponding reference numbers employed, as in the transcriptions of the Latin manuscripts of *VP* (see Jiroušková 2006). In order to highlight the translation procedures and creative re-elaboration of the Latin apocryphon in the edited text, I have noted all secondary additions, repetitions, anticipation and postponement of the original readings with the sigla *add*, *bis*, *inc*, *des*. Variant readings of Copenhagen, Den Arnamagnæanske Samling, AM 681 c 4to, f. 1r (B), which contains less than one-tenth of the original text, are noted in the footnotes.

The Latin text on which the Norse translation is based is composed of a collection of variant readings that best represent the vernacular rendition, which as shown above, seem to be mostly indebted to manuscripts of the C/spec type. When possible, I have included the readings of L^{12}, the

---

[173] Ólafr had been away for three years, as can be gathered from a letter from Hólar dated 18 April 1486 (*DI*, VI 564/10–565/9).

codex that shares the highest number of variants with *PLe*. Whenever L[12] presents deficiencies or divergent readings, I have used the readings of the other manuscripts pertaining to the C/spec group, particularly those of M[5], P[6], P[7] and P[8], and referred to the corresponding reading of L[12] in the footnotes for purposes of comparison. As to the Latin text, I have relied entirely on the transcriptions available in Jiroušková, *Die Visio Pauli* (Jiroušková 2006, 510–931), and for the sake of consistency, I have adopted the same conventions of modern capitalisation and punctuation as those followed for *PLe*.

In order to facilitate readability and comparison with other vernacular translations, the text of *PLe* has been normalised according to the editorial conventions of the *ONP*, which reconstructs a stage of the language from *c*.1200–50. Accordingly, differentiation has been made between the mutated vowels *ǽ* and *ǿ*, which at that stage represented respectively the phonemes /æ:/ and /ø:/. However, in order to present the reader with an impression of the character of AM 624 4to, some of its later features have been retained. Most notably, the manuscript cluster *vo* has been maintained throughout, as in *voru*, *vors* for *váru*, *várs*, rather than being normalised into *vá*; a shift that is observable in manuscripts from the first half of the fourteenth century up to the late Middle Ages. Nevertheless, since the scribe has consistently employed the adverb *svá* in its older form, this conservative trait has been preserved in the edited text. The verb *gøra* and its inflected forms, represented consistently in the manuscript with the digraphs *io*, have been transcribed with the front rounded vowel *ø*. The only exception to this convention is represented by the very last section of the edited text (41/add), in which the verb is found twice written with the palatal vowel *e* as *gerum*, *gera*. Since the palatalisation of *ø* might indicate that this reading was added during a second stage of the textual transmission, the two forms of AM 624 4to have been retained in the edition. Supplied text is indicated within open angle brackets (⟨⟩). Barely legible words are placed within square brackets ([ ]), whereas secondary scribal insertions are placed within single quotation marks (' '). All holes in the manuscripts have been indicated in the footnotes (*foramen in cod.*). Foliation of the manuscript is given within the transcription. Manuscript punctuation and capitalisation of personal names and place names have been normalised according to modern practice. Direct literal quotations from the Bible are highlighted in italics, whereas allusions to the *NHB*, the *IHB*, *DLe* or *Æf* have been left in roman type and are noted in the footnotes. All editorial interventions are signalled in the first person (*emendavi*, *conieci*). Whenever a given reading differs from the texts available in

Tveitane (Tv) or Wellendorf (We),[174] I have noted it in the footnotes.

I have attempted to offer a close translation of the Norse and Latin texts and have departed from the originals only when the sense in modern English would have been compromised. I have also decided to make fairly literal translations of the *hapax legomena* that occur in the text and have left the reference to the soul as a feminine being, 'she/her', as is customary in Norse and Latin (*sál/anima*). Direct quotations from the scriptures are taken verbatim from the Douay–Rheims Bible.

List of Abbreviations

add. = *addidit* [scribal addition]
bis = *bis scripsit* [scribal repetition]
cod. = *codex* [manuscript]
conieci [editorial conjecture (present editor)]
coniecit [editorial conjecture (previous editor)]
corr. = *correxit* [scribal correction]
des = *desinit* [end of a variant]
eras. = *erasit* [scribal erasure]
e. g. = *exempli gratia* [for example]
emendavi [editorial emendation]
foramen in cod. [hole in the manuscript]
inc = *incipit* [beginning of a variant]
lect. dub. = *lectio dubita* [dubious reading]
om. = *omisit* [scribal omission]

---

[174] *En norrøn versjon av Visio Pauli* 1964, 8–13 and Wellendorf 2009, 411–15.

PÁLS LEIZLA

DE VISIONE SANCTI PAULI

THE VISION OF ST PAUL

ON THE VISION OF ST PAUL

Páls leizla. De visione Sancti Pauli

⟨PÁLS LEIZLA⟩

12a
pons

[**147r**] ⟨Ok brú liggr yfir á⟩na ok ganga þar yfir góðra manna sálir án allri hræzlu en synðugra manna sálir ganga mjǫk hræddar ok skulu þær af falla brúni ok ganga sumar lengra en sumar skemmra.

12b
mansiones

Ok skulu[1] í þeirri á brenna í eldi líkr meðr líkum en illr meðr illum.

14
dimersi

Sumir standa[2] í þeirri á til nafla eða til knjá sumir undir hendr sumir undir hǫku sumir til varra en sumir til brúna ok hvern dag eru þeir eilífliga píndir.

14a
dimersi ad
genua

Þa komsk[3] Páll postoli við ok klǫkk vesǫld þeirra ok eymd ok spurði engil hverju þetta gegnði eða sætti. En eingill sagði honum. Þeir menn sem standa til knj[á][4] eru þeir sem bakmálugir[5] voru ok gótt þótti[6] margt at mæla um aðra

---

[1] skulu] *emendavi* skal, skal Tv, We
[2] standa] *emendavi* standa til, standa We, standa til Tv
[3] komsk] komz Tv, komsk We
[4] knj[á] *foramen in cod.*
[5] bakmálugir] bakmálgir We
[6] þótti] þótti Tv, þóttu We

DE VISIONE SANCTI PAULI[1]

[Et super illud flumem est] pons et super[2] illum transiunt anime iuste sine ulla dubitacione et peccatrices unaqueque secundum meritum.[3,4]

Ibi sunt mansiones multe preparate sicut dicit Dominus in Evangelio. *Ligate per fasciculos ad comburendum*[5] id est similes cum similibus adulteros cum adulteris raptores cum rapacibus iniquos cum iniquis.[6]

Ibi vidit Paulus multas animas demersas. Alias usque ad genua alias usque ad umbilicum alias usque ad labia alias usque ad supercilia et cotidie perhenniter cruciantur.[7]

Et flevit Paulus et suspiravit[8] interrogans angelum qui essent qui mersi fuerant usque ad genua. Cui angelus ait. Hii sunt qui inmittunt se sermonibus alienis alios detrahentes.[9]

---

[1] L[12]
[2] super] per C/spec
[3] *post* meritum *add.* suum C/spec
[4] L[12]
[5] Mat 13:30
[6] L[12], L[9], M[5] P[6], P[8]
[7] L[12], M[5], P[6], P[7], P[8]
[8] suspiravit] *om.* C/spec
[9] L[12]

	THE VISION OF ST PAUL	ON THE VISION OF ST PAUL
12a *bridge*	[**147r**] And a bridge lies over the river and the souls of good people walk over it without any fear whatsoever and the souls of sinful people walk much afraid, and they shall fall off the bridge and some walk a greater distance and some a shorter.	And over that river there is a bridge and the righteous souls cross over it without any uncertainty and [so do] the sinful, each according to merit.
12b *abodes*	And in that river they shall burn in the fire, like with like and evil with evil.	In that place many abodes are prepared, as the Lord says in the Gospel: *Bind it unto bundles to burn*, that is like with like, adulterous with adulterous, thieves with the greedy of plunder, unjust with unjust.
14 *plunged*	In that river some stand up to the navel or up to the knees, some up to the armpits, some up to the chin, some up to the lips and some up to the eyebrows, and every day they are tortured eternally.	In that place Paul saw many souls plunged: some up to the knees, others up to the navel, others up to the lips, others up to the eyebrows, and every day they were tortured perpetually.
14a *plunged up to the knees*	Then the apostle Paul was moved and sobbed for their misery and wretchedness and asked the angel what was the cause and the reason for it. And the angel said to him: 'Those people who stand up to the knees are those who were backbiters and thought it good to speak with howls about others and they made	And Paul wept and sighed and asked the angel who those were, who were plunged up to their knees, to which the angel said: 'They are those who joined in other people's conversations and slandered others.

4 Páls leizla. De visione Sancti Pauli

munskvaldur ok [ó]hljóðun[7] gørðu í kirkju þá er hin helga messa var sungin.

14b *dimersi ad umbilicum*

En þeir menn er til nafla standa voru hórd[ómsmenn][8] ok átu ofmikit ok drukku ok eigi vildu láta hungra sik fyrir Guðs sakir.

Qui ad umbilicum sunt fornicatores et adulterantes qui postea non redeunt[10] ad penitenciam.[11]

14c *dimersi ad labia (!)*

En þeir er undir hendr standa ræntu ok stálu jafnkristna sér.

Qui ad labia[12] hii sunt qui faciunt lites in ecclesia inter se non audientes verbum Dei.[13]

14d *dimersi ad supercilia (!)*

En þeir er undir hǫku[9] standa svíkja annan til lífs ok fjár.

Alii usque ad supercilia hii sunt traditores[14] qui gaudent super malicia proximorum.[15]

14c/bis *dimersi ad labia*

En þeir er til munns standa lifðu[10] eftir munaðarráði[11] ok ei þyrmdu fǫður ok móður í illum orðum ok fyrirlétu Guðs orð ok helga trú.

Qui ad labia hii sunt qui faciunt lites in ecclesia inter se non audientes verbum Dei.[16]

14d/bis *dimersi ad supercilia*

En þeir ⟨er⟩ til brúna standa bǫrðu fǫður sinn ok móður ok sóru eiða ranga ok myrðu menn til fjár sér ok tóku fé illa eðr ræntu kirkjur ok eigi villdu fyrergefa ǫðrum ok eigi vildu til skriftar [ganga né yf⟨irb⟩ǿta].[12]

Qui ad supercilia hii sunt qui gaudent super malicia proximorum.[17]

18a/inc *peccata (usuras querunt)*

⟨Ok svá⟩[13] sagði engill.

De quibus ait angelus.[18]

---

[7] [ó]hljóðun *foramen in cod.*
[8] hórd[ómsmenn] *foramen in cod.*
[9] hǫku] supercilia C mss.
[10] lifðu] *emendavi* lifði, lifðu We, lifði Tv
[11] munaðarráði] múnaðar ráði We, Tv
[12] yf⟨irb⟩ǿta *foramen in cod.*
[13] ⟨Ok svá⟩ *om.* Tv, We

[10] redeunt] recordantur C/spec
[11] L[12]
[12] labia] C mss. cf. *e.g.* brachia L[5]
[13] L[12], M[5], P[6], P[7], P[8]
[14] hii sunt traditores] *om.* L[12]
[15] M[5], P[6], P[7], P[8]
[16] L[12], M[5], P[6], P[7], P[8]
[17] L[12], D[2], M[5], P[6], P[7], P[8]
[18] De quibus ait angelus] 20c, 24a C/spec

	noise in church while the holy mass was sung.	
14b *plunged up to the navel*	And those people who stand up to the navel were adulterers and ate and drank excessively and were not willing to go hungry for the sake of God.	Those who are up to the navel are fornicators and adulterers who thereafter did not turn to penance.
14c *plunged up to the lips (!)*	And those who stand up to the armpits pillaged and stole from their fellow Christians.	Those who are up to their lips are those who fight with each other at Church not listening to the Word of God.
14d *plunged up to the eyebrows (!)*	And those who stand up to their chins cheat other people of life and property.	Others up to their eyebrows are traitors who rejoice in the wickedness of neighbours.
14c/bis *plunged up to the lips*	And those who stand up to their mouths lived according to the counsel of desire and they would not spare [their] fathers and mothers from evil words and abandoned the Word of God and the Holy Faith.	Those up to their lips are those who fight with each other at church not listening to the Word of God.
14d/bis *plunged up to the eyebrows*	And those who stand up to the eyebrows beat their fathers and mothers and swore false oaths and murdered people to gain wealth for themselves and took money in an evil manner or pillaged churches and were not willing to forgive others and were not willing to confess and do penance.'	Those up to their eyebrows are those who rejoice in the wickedness of neighbours.'
18a/inc *sins* *(seek to obtain usuries)*	And so the angel said.	To these things, the angel said.

Páls leizla. De visione Sancti Pauli

18 *viri et mulieres linguas comedentes*	Því næst komu þau í þann stað [er][14] ⟨menn ok konur⟩[15] átu tungur[16] sínar.	Deinde vidit alium locum tenebrosum plenum viris et mulieribus commedentibus linguas suas.[19 20]
18a *peccata (usuras querunt)*	Þessir eru þeir <...>[17] er seldu á leigu orð sín ok tóku við mútum ok voru ómiskunnsamir við þurfamenn blótrífir ok gauðrífir eru.	Hii feneratores pecuniarum qui usuras querunt et non sunt misericordes proptea sunt in pena.[21]
20 *omnes pene*	Nú komu þeir í þann stað	Et vidit alium locum in quo omnes pene erant.[22]
20a *puelle nigre indute pice et sulphure*	er konur ungar ok margar voru. Þǽr voru í bikaðum [ky]rtlum[18] brunnu þǽr innan en frøru útan ormar ok pǫddr hrøktu [þ]ǽr[19] sárliga.	Et ibi puelle nigre habentes nigra vestimenta indute pice et sulphure et draconibus igneis serpentibus atque viperis circa colla sua.[23]
20b *angeli quattor*	En fjándr stǫnguðu þǽr með spjótum en sumir bǫrðu með vǫndum.	Et erant quattor angeli maligni ibi increpantes eas habentes cornua ignita qui ibant in circuitu earum dicentes. Agnoscite Filium Dei qui redemit mundum.[24]
20c *peccata (castitatem non servantes infantes nacaverunt)*	Þá spurði Páll postoli hvat þǽr hǫfðu gǫrt til svá mikla písla. E⟨n⟩gill svarar honom. Þessar saurguðusk undir frǽndr sína ok gǫrðu hórdóm undir bǿndr sína ok drápu á	Et interrogavit Paulus que essent. Tunc respondit angelus. Hee sunt que non servaverunt castitatem usque ad nupcias et maculaverunt se cum parentibus suis et necaverunt infantes suos et dederunt porcis in escam vel canibus et

---

[14] [er] *foramen in cod.*
[15] [er] ⟨menn ok konur⟩] *conieci* viris et mulieribus, er [menn] Tv, We
[16] tungur] *emendavi* tungar, tungar We, tungur Tv
[17] <...> 18a/inc.
[18] [ky]rtlum *foramen in cod.*
[19] [þ]ǽr *foramen in cod., om.* Tv, We

---

[19] Deinde vidit ... / ... linguas suas] 20c, 24a C/spec
[20] L^{12}, L^4, Sch
[21] L^{12}, L^4, Sch, Br
[22] L^{12}, Sch, Br
[23] L^{12}, L^9, M^5, P^7, P^8, L^4
[24] L^{12}, D^2, M^5, P^6, P^7, P^8, Sch, L^4, Br

18 *men and women eating their tongues*	Thereafter they arrived in that place where men and women ate their own tongues:	Thereupon he saw another gloomy place full of men and women eating their [own] tongues:
18a *sins (seek to obtain usuries)*	'These are they <. . .>¹ who hired out their words and took bribes and were unmerciful towards needy men; they are eager for curse and eager for abuse.'	'They are usurers of money who sought usuries and are not merciful; for this reason they undergo punishment.'
20 *all punishments*	Then they arrived in that place	And he saw another place in which there were all punishments.
20a *black maidens covered with pitch and sulphur*	where there were many young women. They were clothed in pitch tunics; they burned inside and froze outside. Snakes and toads persecuted them sorely.	And there were black maidens [clothed] with black vestments covered with pitch and sulphur and with fiery snakes and serpents and vipers around their necks.
20b *four angels*	And devils goaded them with spears and some beat them with wands.	And there were four wicked angels rebuking them holding ignited horns who went around them in a circle saying: 'Acknowledge the Son of God who has redeemed the world!'
20c *sins (did not maintain chastity, murdered new-born)*	Then the apostle Paul asked what they had done to [deserve] such great tortures. The angel answers him: 'These defiled themselves under their male relatives and practised adultery against their husbands and secretly killed their children and are	And Paul asked who they were. Then the angel replied: 'They are those who did not maintain chastity until their marriages and defiled themselves with their relatives and murdered their new-borns and gave [them] as food to swine and dogs

---

¹ <...> 18a/inc

laun bǫrn sín ok þǽr ⟨eru⟩²⁰ [**147v**] konur er fé tóku á sér. Þat voru pútur ok eigi iðraðusk fyrir dauðan.

28f
viri et mulieres nudi et vermes

Þá komu þeir í þann stað er menn átu forska pǫddur ok nǫðrur²¹ ok allskyns kvikvendi.

24a
peccatores

Þá spurði²² Páll postoli hvat þǽr hǫfðu gǫrt. Þá svaraði engill: Þessir menn átu ok drukku á hátíðum ok sátu í mǫrgum drykkjum ok vildu²³ eigi hlýða þá er hin helga messa var sungin ok vildu eigi fasta ok voru offastir af fé sínu við fátøka menn ok helga staði. ⟨Þ⟩á gengu þau en ok fundu hús mikit²⁴ ok sá í því menn marga ok alla nøkta ok voru sumt konur en sumt karlmenn ok voru illa píndir af frost[i]²⁵ ok eldi. Paulus spyrr. Hvat gørðu þessir menn til svá mikla písla. Engill svarar. Þessir menn

Et vidit in alio loco viros ac mulieres et vermes et serpentes commedentes eos. Et erant anime vive²⁷ <...> alteram quasi oves in ovili.²⁸

Et interrogavit Paulus qui essent. Et dixit angelus.²⁹ Hii sunt qui ieiunia ante tempus despiciunt. Et postea vidit Paulus viros et mulieres in loco glaciali et ignis urebat mediam partem eorum et alia pars frigescebat. Et interrogavit Paulus qui essent. Et dixit angelus. Hii sunt qui orphanis et viduis iniuste nocuerunt ac etiam eos contra iusticiam opresserunt et postea cum eis non concordabantur.³⁰³¹

proiecerunt in fluminibus et in aliis perdicionibus et postea penitenciam non egerunt.²⁵²⁶

---

²⁰ ⟨eru⟩ *om.* Tv, We
²¹ forska pǫddur ok nǫðrur] cf. ormmum pauddum ok froskum DL 4/21 (A)
²² spurði] *emendavi* spurðu, spurðu Tv, We
²³ vildu] *emendavi* vildi, villdi Tv, vildu We
²⁴ Þá gengu þau en ok fundu hús mikit] cf. þa syndiz þeim hus opit ok suo mikid sem hit mesta fiall DL 47/12-13 (A)
²⁵ frost[i] *foramen in cod.*

²⁵ *add.* 18a C/spec
²⁶ L¹², Sch
²⁷ vive *om.* C/spec
²⁸ L¹²
²⁹ Et interrogavit . . . / . . . angelus] Et de illum dictum est L¹²
³⁰ ac etiam . . . / . . . non concordabantur] *om.* C/spec
³¹ D²

(On) The Vision of Saint Paul

	[those] women who took money for themselves. These were harlots and did not repent before death.'	and abandoned [them] in rivers and [in] other [places of] perdition and thereafter they did not do penance.'
28f *naked men and women and worms*	Then they arrived in that place where people ate frogs, toads and adders, and all kind of living creatures.	And in another place he saw men and women and worms and serpents eating them and the souls were living [one above] the other almost like sheep in a sheepfold.
24a *sinners*	Then Paul the apostle asked what they had done. The angel answered: 'These people ate and drank on feast days and sat at many banquets and were not willing to harken while the holy mass was sung and did not wish to fast and were too tight with their money towards poor men and holy places.' Then they proceeded further and found a great house and in it they saw many people all naked, some were women and some men, and they were badly tormented by frost and fire. Paul asks what these people did [to earn] such great tortures. The angel answers: 'These people	And Paul asked who they were. And the angel said: 'They are those who disdained fasting before time.' And thereafter Paul saw men and women in an icy location, and fire burnt them on one side and the other side grew cold. And Paul asked who they were, and the angel said: 'They are those who did harm to orphans and widows unjustly and also oppressed them [going] against justice and thereafter would not come to agreement with them.'

Páls leizla. *De visione Sancti Pauli*

vildu eigi gefa fyrer Guðs²⁶ sakir klǽði né skúa ok eigi mat né drykk ok létusk eigi sjá né vita vesǫld né eymð fátøka manna fǫðurlausra barna ekkna ok kvenna forstǫðulausra ok ekki vildu hjalpa frǽndum sínum ok vísuðu ór herbergjum sínum þurfamǫnnum.

26
senex inter diabolos

⟨Þ⟩á komu þeir í þann stað er maðr stóð við stiku ok tunga hans ⟨var⟩²⁷ dregin út ʼinn um kverkr honum´ ok negld við stikuna ok stóðu við fjándr ok bǫrðu hana meðr járnvǫlum.

Mox vidit in alio loco unum senem inter quatuor diabolos plorantem et ululantem.

26a/des
peccata eius

Þá spurði postolinn. Því sjá maðr þoldi svá mikla pínu.

Et interrogavit Paulus quis esset.³²

26a
peccata eius

Engill svarar. Þessi²⁸ maðrinn ok hverr annara e⟨r⟩ svá eru píndir voru illir í tungu ok²⁹ báru skjótvitni ok þeir er því ǫllu er frǽndr urðu fjándmenn ok vínir [hró]parar³⁰ voru af hans róg[i]³¹ ok margyrðum ok svá gramdi hann Guð at sér með sinni tungu þá er³² hann sór ósǿra eiða ok mǽlti ⟨illt⟩ við fǫður sinn ok móður brǿðr ok sýstur eða presta eða kennimenn þá er messur syngja ok fóru

Et dixit angelus. Episcopus negligens fuit non custodivit legem Dei non fuit castus corpore nec cogitacione nec verbo nec opere sed fuit avarus et dolosus atque superbus.³³ ³⁴

---

²⁶ Guðs] Guð, Guðs Tv
²⁷ ⟨var⟩ *om.* Tv, We
²⁸ þessi] *emendavi* þisse
²⁹ ok] um Tv, We
³⁰ hró]parar *eras. in cod.*
³¹ róg[i] *eras. in cod.*
³² er] *om.* Tv, We

---

³² L¹², D², P⁶, P⁷
³³ *post* superbus *add.* ideo sustinet innumerabiles penas usque in diem iudicii C/spec
³⁴ L¹², D², L⁹, M⁵, P⁶, P⁷, P⁸

(On) The Vision of Saint Paul

were not willing to give either clothes or shoes for the sake of God and either food or drink and would not allow themselves either to see or to be conscious of the misery or the wail of poor men, fatherless children, widows and women without protection and were not willing to help their relatives, nor did they show needy men [the way] out of their lodgings.'

26
an old man among devils

Then they arrived in that place where a man stood by a stake and [had] his tongue drawn out through his throat and nailed to the stake and the devils stood by and beat her [the soul] with iron rods.

Afterwards in another place he saw an old man crying and howling among four devils.

26a/des
his sins

Then the apostle asked why this man endured such a great torture.

And Paul asked who he was.

26a
his sins

The Angel answers: 'This man and all others who are punished in this way were evil in tongue and bore hasty witness. And they are those who made relatives and friends [their] enemies and they were defamers of his slander and calumny. He [this man] made God so angry against himself with his tongue when he committed perjuries[2] and spoke evil

And the angel said: 'He was a careless bishop. He did not observe the Law of God. He was neither pure in the body nor in the thought.'

---

[2] Literally 'he swore unswearable oaths'

26a/add
peccata eius

með lygi ok lausung manna í millum.

En komu þeir í þann stað [er]³³ menn voru grafnir ⟨í⟩ jǫrð niðr undir hendr ok var lagðr á herðar þeim eldr ok á ketill ok voru þar í sálir kristna manna ok vall sem mátti. Þá spyrr Páll postoli hvat þessir menn hefði gørt. Engill svarar. Þeir voru Dróttins svíkarar réntu heilaga kirkju drápu biskupa ok lærða menn aðra³⁴ ok bǫrðu fǫður ok móður eða systkin eða skylda fr[148r]⟨æ⟩ndr sína ok fóru með galdra ok gørningar eða fyrirgørðu mǫnnum eða búfé af fjándans krafti.

27a
Ve ve peccatoribus!

Þá mælti Páll postoli. Vei vei yðr syndugum mǫnnum. Ósýnju voru³⁵ þeir bornir í heimin.

Tunc flevit Paulus et dixit. Ve ve peccatoribus. Ut quid nati sunt.³⁵ ³⁶

27b
Quid ploras? Nondum vidisti maiora supplicia

Þá svaraði engill. Því lætr þú svá aumliga at þessara manna sálum ok píslum. Eigi hefir þú en sét þeirra manna píslir er mestar eru í helvíti.

Et dixit angelus. Quid fles, Paule. Nondum vidisti maiores pęnas inferni.³⁷ ³⁸

---

³³ [er] *foramen in cod.*

³⁴ réntu heilaga kirkju, drápu biskupa ok lærða menn aðra] cf. þa mællti salin huad kallar þu kirkiu stuld eingellinn mællti þad sem stolid er ok uikt til *Gwds þionozstu er haft. Bækr edr messo klædi ok kalekar edr annad þess konar pijng edr þo at oheilagt sie þegar ur kirkiu er stolid DL 42/10-14 (A)

³⁵ voru] voro Tv, várud We

³⁵ Tunc flevit . . . / . . . nati sunt?] Et flevit Paulus et suspiravit C/spec, *om.* L¹²

³⁶ D⁴, C⁶

³⁷ Et dixit angelus . . . / . . . maiores pęnas inferni] *om.* L¹²

³⁸ M⁵, P⁶, P⁷, P⁸

against his father, mother, brothers and sisters or to the priests who sing masses. And [men like him] went about with lies and falsehood among people.'

26a/add *his sins*	Then they arrived in that place where men were buried beneath the earth up to their armpits and on their shoulders was laid a fire and on [it] a cauldron and in it there were the souls of Christians and it bubbled mightily. Then the apostle Paul asks what these people had done. The angel answers: 'They were betrayers of God, they pillaged the Holy Church and killed bishops and other learned men and beat their fathers and mothers or siblings or they oppress [their] relatives. And they practised spells and sorcery and bewitched people or livestock by the power of the devil.'	
27a *Woe woe to the sinners!*	Then the apostle Paul said: 'Woe, woe to you sinful people! Unfittingly they were born into the world!'	Then Paul wept and said: 'Woe, woe to sinners! Wherefore are they born?'
27b *Why do you wail? You have not yet seen the greater punishments*	Then the angel answered: 'Why do you suffer so miserably for the souls and tortures of these people? You have not yet seen those people's tortures that are the greatest in Hell.'	And the angel said: 'Why do you wail, O Paul? You have not yet seen the greater punishments of Hell.'

14 Páls leizla. De visione Sancti Pauli

28
puteus sigillatus

⟨Þ⟩á leiddi hann postolan at sjá einn brunn með VII innsiglum. Þá mælti engill við postolan at hann skyldi standa langt frá at hann mætti standask þá hinu mikla³⁶ óþefan er þaðan er laust ór þeim hinu fúla brunni.

Et ostendit puteum septem sigillis signatum et ait illi. Sta alonge ut possit³⁹ sustinere fetorem.⁴⁰

28a
fetor

En ór þessum hinum fúla pytt ok illa þá laust svá illum þef at hann var verri en allar aðrar helvítis kvalar.

Tunc aperto puteo surrexit fetor malus superans omnes penas inferni.⁴¹⁴²

28d
commemoracio Dei

Ok en sagði engill svá at hverr þeirra er í þenna pytt fellr sá á aldri von til Guðs.

Et ait angelus. Si quis inciderit⁴³ in puteum istum numquam erit commemoracio de eo in conspectu Dei.⁴⁴

28e
peccata

Þá svarar Páll postoli. Hverir eru þeir er svá eru aumir. Michael engil⟨l⟩ svarar. Þeir sem eigi vildu trúa á Guð almáttigan ok þeir sem tǫluðu lygi at Guð væri Faðir ok Sonr ok Heilagr Andi ok því at hann sé af Helgum Anda³⁷ ok borinn af Maríu meyju ok ei trúðu burð Krists né upprísu hans ok því at hann væri krossfestr ok þeir er ⟨eigi⟩³⁸ tóku við trú ok kristni ok heldu eigi síðan ok eigi vildu taka hold ok blóð Drottins Vors Ihesu Christi ok ⟨eigi⟩ vildu til skriftar ganga.

Et ait Paulus.⁴⁵ Qui sunt qui mittuntur in eo. Et dixit angelus. Hi sunt qui non credunt Christum Filium Dei venisse in carne nec nasci de Maria virgine et qui non sunt baptizati nec communicati de corpore et sanguine Christi.⁴⁶

---

³⁶ mikla] *emendavi* miklu, miklu Tv, mikla We
³⁷ Anda] Tv anda, We andi,
³⁸ ⟨eigi⟩ *om.* Tv, We

---

³⁹ ut possit] ut possis C/spec
⁴⁰ M⁵
⁴¹ superans omnes penas inferni] et multa vilia eiecit horribilia C/spec mss
⁴² L¹², L⁴
⁴³ inciderit] mittutur C/spec, *om.* L¹²
⁴⁴ C6, D4
⁴⁵ Paulus] angelus L¹²
⁴⁶ M⁵, L⁹, P⁸

28 *a sealed pit*	Then he led the apostle to see a well with seven seals. Then the angel told the apostle that he should stand far away from [it] so that he could bear the great stench that came from there, out of that foul well.	And he showed a pit sealed with seven seals and said to him: 'Stay far off!' so that he could bear the stench.
28a *stench*	And from that foul and evil pit came such an evil stench that it was worse than all the other pains of Hell.	Then once the pit was opened there came up a bad stench, which exceeded all the pains of Hell.
28d *God's remembrance*	And then the angel said that each of those that fall into that pit will never have hope of God.	And the angel said: 'If anyone falls into this pit there shall never be any remembrance of him before God.'
28e *sins*	Then the apostle Paul answers: 'Who are these who are so miserable?' The angel Michael answers: 'Those who were not willing to believe in God Almighty and those who called it a lie that God was the Father, the Son and the Holy Spirit, and that He proceeds from the Holy Spirit and [is] born of the Virgin Mary. And they did not believe in the birth of Christ nor in His resurrection and that He was crucified. And [they are] those who did not accept the faith and Christianity or that subsequently did not maintain it and did not wish to take the flesh and blood of Our Lord Jesus Christ and were not willing to go to confession.'	And Paul said: 'Who are these who are sent into it?' And the angel said: 'They are those who do not believe that Christ the Son came in the flesh nor that He is born from the Virgin Mary and who have neither been baptised nor taken communion of the Body and Blood of Christ.'

16 Páls leizla. De visione Sancti Pauli

28f/bis
viri et mulieres nudi et vermes

Nú komu þeir í þann stað er voru konar ok karlar ok þoldu illar píslir ǿptu sem hǽst ok hǫfðu mikla rǫdd ok hrǽðiliga. Ok var þar leiðiligr krytr ok grátr óp ok gabb ok gnístan tanna.³⁹

Et vidit in alio loco viros ac mulieres⁴⁷ et vermes et serpentes commedentes eos. Et erant anime vive <...> alteram quasi oves in ovili.⁴⁸

28f/add
viri et mulieres nudi et vermes

Þeir menn voru brendir á báli ok sindranda grjóti ok aumliga veldir ok barðir með sleggjum. En suma rífu vargar ok hundar í sundr. En suma hjoggu ormar ok nǫðrur⁴⁰ ok svá illa kvaldar at þat fǽr engi talit né tínt mannligri tungu at ei þyldi þat folk fleira ok verra.

28g
profunditas loci

Ok voru þǽr sálir í svá djúpum stað sem er í milli [h]imins⁴¹ ⟨ok⟩ jarðar.

Et erat profunditas loci⁴⁹ quasi exaltantur celi a terra⁵⁰ et audivit gemitum et suspirium magnum quasi tonitruum.⁵¹

28g/add
profunditas loci

Ok sagði engill at þat voru bannsettir menn þeir sem Guð píndu ok í hǫfuðsyndum ok glǿpum voru ok vildu eigi afláta né yfirbǿta né

---

³⁹ ok gnístan tanna] cf. og tanna skialfti DL 50/13 (Λ)
⁴⁰ En suma rífu vargar ok hundar í sundr. En suma hjoggu ormar ok nǫðrur] cf. þar þolde sw enn auma saal. hunda bit ok warga slit. barnijngar ok biarnar bit ok leona ok fleiri annara dyra. orma haugg ok eitr naudror ok margra annara grimligra ok ogurliga dyra DL 36/21-37/10 (A)
⁴¹ [h]imins *foramen in cod.*

⁴⁷ Et vidit in alio loco viros ac mulieres] Postea Paulus aspicebat in celum et in terram et vidit alium locum tenebrosum plenum viris et muliribus. Et una anima super aliam volutabatur quasi oves in ovile C/spec
⁴⁸ L¹²
⁴⁹ lacus *in cod.*
⁵⁰ Et erat profunditas locus quasi exaltantur celi a terra] *om.* C/spec
⁵¹ L¹², L⁴

(On) The Vision of Saint Paul

28f/bis *naked men and women and worms*	Now they arrived in the place where there were women and men who endured terrible tortures and screamed loudly and had loud and frightened voices. And there was horrible murmuring and weeping, cries, jeers and gnashing of teeth.	And in another place he saw men and women and worms and serpents eating them. And the souls were alive <. . .> [one upon] the other almost like sheep in a sheepfold.
28f/add *naked men and women and worms*	These people were burnt at the stake and on a glowing stone, sorely boiled and beaten with sledge-hammers. And wolves and hounds ripped some asunder and snakes and adders bit some [others] and tormented [them] so severely that nothing so bad can be told or recounted with human language that these people did not endure more and worse.	
28g *depth of the location*	And these souls were in a place so deep that it is between heaven and earth.	And the depth of the location was as if the heavens deepened on earth, and he heard a groan and a great sigh as if it were thunder.
28g/add *depth of the location*	And the angel said that those were excommunicated people who had tormented God and engaged in capital sins and misdeeds and wished neither to remit nor repent	

sættask við Guð. Ok þeir er ørvilnaðusk Guðs miskunna ok aldri vildu fyrirgefa ǫðrum misgerðir.

30
anima peccatoris

Ok þá sá postolinn [**148v**] borna sál syndogs manns til helvítis ok fylgðo VII englar fjándans ok fóru með hana illa ok bǫrðu hana ok brugðu brigslum.⁴²

Et postea aspiciebat inter celum et terram et vidit animam peccatoris⁵² ululantem inter septem diabolos deducentes eam cotidie de corpore egressam.⁵³

30a
clamor angelorum

Ok mæltu svá við hana. Vei verði þér syndug sála aum ok vesǫl ertu. Á vorrar fortǫlur hlýddir þú þér mjǫg óhagligar ok eigi gørðir þú þurftir þínar meðan þú máttir bjarga þér hér í v[er]ǫldinni.⁴³

Et clamaverunt contra eam angeli male dicens. Ve ve tibi, anima misera. Que operata es male in terra?⁵⁴ ⁵⁵

32
anima iusti

Þá sá hann aðra sál borna til himinríkis.

Post hec vidit Paulus angelos ducentes animam cuiusdam sancti sacerdotis in celum de corpore tunc exeuntem.⁵⁶ ⁵⁷

32a
vox angelorum

Ok fylgðu henne VII englar Guðs með sǫng ok dýrðligri rǫdd ok óumrǿðiligum fagnaði ok gleði ok mæltu þeir við sálina. Gleðsk þú hin helga því at þú gørðir þíns Dróttins vilja ok alldri skáltu þína samvist við hana skilja.

Et audiunt vocem milium angelorum⁵⁸ letancium et dicencium. O beata anima o felicissima sponsa o beata

---

⁴² bǫrðu hana ok brugðu brigslum] cf. hurfo þeir um hana ok brixlodo henne synda brixle DL 50/8-10 (A)

⁴³ v[er]ǫldinni *foramen in cod.*

⁵² animam peccatoris] animam peccatricem C/spec

⁵³ L¹², L⁴, Br

⁵⁴ Que operata es male in terra?] *om.* C/spec

⁵⁵ L¹², P⁶, Br

⁵⁶ Post hec vidit Paulus angelos . . . / . . . tunc exeunte] Post hec adduxerunt angeli animam iusti de corpore portantes eam ad celum C/spec

⁵⁷ L¹²

⁵⁸ vocem milium angelorum] *om.* C/spec

(On) The Vision of Saint Paul

nor be reconciled with God. And those who [now] despaired of the mercy of God and were never willing to forgive the offences of others.

30
the soul of a sinner

And then the apostle saw the soul of a sinful man being brought to Hell and seven angels of the devil accompanied it and treated it badly, beat it and upbraided it with reproaches.

And thereafter he looked between heaven and earth and he saw the soul of a sinner, which stepped daily out of the body and howled among seven devils, who were leading it away.

30a
cry of the angels

And they spoke thus to it: 'Woe to you, sinful soul, you are poor and miserable! But you have given heed to our exhortations much less opportunely and you did not fulfil your obligations while you could have saved yourself here in this world.'

And against it the angels cried out cruelly saying: 'Woe, woe to you, miserable soul! Why have you acted wickedly on earth?'

32
the soul of a just man

Then he saw another soul being brought into heaven.

Thereafter Paul saw angels leading a soul of a certain holy priest into heaven, which was then departing from the body.

32a
voice of angels

And seven angels of God accompany her with song and a glorious voice and an indescribable joy and happiness and they said to the soul: 'Rejoice, you holy one, since you have done the will of your Lord and your dwelling with it shall never be parted,

And they hear the voice of a thousand rejoicing angels saying: 'O blessed soul, o happiest bride! O blessed in

Páls leizla. De visione Sancti Pauli

32a/add
vox angelorum

Því at þú skildir líkam þinn frá mǫrgu því er honom þótti gótt at hafa ok gørðir þat fyrir Guðs sakir. Þess skaltu nú njóta ok taka þá sælu á móti er engi kann frá at segja ok er sú sæla endalaus.

in Christo letare quia fecisti hodie voluntatem Dei tui.[59]

33b
miserere I (Michael et Paule)

Þá ǿptu syndroga manna sálir er í helvíti voru með aumligri rǫddu ok mæltu svá. Miskunna miskunna.

Et clamaverunt peccatores in inferno[60] dicentes. Miserere nobis Michael archangele et tu Paule dilectissime Dei intercede pro nobis ad Dominum.[61]

33c
angelus ait

Michael ok Páll postoli heyrðu til hversu aumliga þessar sálir grétu ok báðu.

Et ait angelus. Nunc flete et flebimus vobiscum et qui mecum sunt angeli cum dilectissimo Paulo ut forte miseratur vestri Deus et donet vobis refrigerium.[62][63]

33d
miserere II (audientes hec)

Síðan báðu þær þessum orðum. Michael ok Páll postoli. Miskunna miskunna Guðs vesligum sálum ok veit þeim nǫkkra hjálp ok miskunn.

Audientes autem hec qui erant in penis exclamaverunt una voce dicentes. Michael archangele et Paule apostole et mila milium angelorum laudancium Deum intercedite

---

[59] L[12]
[60] peccatores in inferno] omnes qui erant in penis C/spec; peccatores qui erant in penis L[12]
[61] L[4], L[12]
[62] ut forte miseratur vestri deus et donet vobis refrigerium] ut suis orationibus det deus vobis refrigerium C/spec
[63] L[12], L[4]

(On) The Vision of Saint Paul

		Christ, rejoice, since today you have done the will of your God!'
32a/add *voice of angels*	since you parted from much that your body liked to have and you did that for God's sake. You shall now benefit from this and receive in return the bliss that none can tell of, and that bliss is endless.'	
33b *Be merciful I (Michael and Paul)*	Then the souls of the sinful people who were in Hell cried out with a miserable voice and spoke thus: 'Have mercy, have mercy!'	And the sinners in Hell cried out saying: 'Be merciful on us! O Archangel Michael and you most beloved Paul, intercede for us with the Lord!'
33c *the angel said*	Michael and the apostle Paul heard how miserably those souls wept and begged.	And the angel said: 'Now weep and we shall weep with you. The angels and the most beloved Paul are with me so that perhaps God may have mercy on you and grant you a respite.'
33d *Be merciful II (hearing this)*	Then they begged with these words: 'Michael and Apostle Paul, have mercy, have mercy on God's poor souls and grant them some help and mercy.'	Hearing them, those who were in pain exclaimed with one voice saying: 'O Archangel Michael and Apostle Paul and the thousands of thousands of angels praising God, intercede for us

Páls leizla. De visione Sancti Pauli

		pro nobis miseris[64] dicentes.[65] Ihesu Christe miserere filiis hominum. Tunc audite sono eorum in quarto celo.[66]
34b *vox Christi I*	Ok þá svarar dróttinlig rǫdd svá mælandi.	Et vox Filii Dei[67] audita est eis per omnes penas dicens. Qui bene non fecistis quare postulastis a me requiem.[68]
34c *vox Christi II*	Ek var krossfestr fyrir yðrar sakir ok ek var þremr nǫglum negldr.[44] Mér var gefit eitr at drekka ok ek þoldi háðuligar hrakningar ok ⟨varð⟩[45] við verði seldr. Síðan þoldi ek drap ok dauða fyrir yðr at þér skylduð vera með mér í eilífum fagnadi.	Ego crucifixus fui pro vobis lancea vulneratus clavis confixus acetum cum felle mixtum dedistis mihi bibere. Ego me ipsum dedi pro vobis in martyrium ut viveretis mecum.[69] [70]
34d *vox Christi III*	En þér létud í móti koma lygi ok lausung dramb ok manndrap ok ágirni ok ǫfund skrǫkvitni ok munneiða hórdóm ok lostasemi hlátr ok skelki, ofát[46] ok ofdrykkju, leti ok líkamsmunuð, mikillæti,[47] blót ok bann ok	Et vos mendaces in vita vestra fuistis et fures et avari et invidi et superbi et maledicti et odium habuistis contra proximos vestros nec decimam rectam dedistis nec sanctam

[44] þremr nauglum negldur] cf. þrimr naofnum næmdr NHB 144/5, IHB 18v/16

[45] ⟨varð⟩ *coniecit* Tv, We

[46] ofat] otátt We

[47] lygi ok lausung dramb ok manndrap ok ágirni ok ǫfund skrǫkvitni ok munneiða hórdóm ok lostasemi hlátr ok skelki ofát ok ofdrykkju leti ok líkamsmunuð mikillìti] cf. *e.g.* við mandrape ok við hordome. við ftuldum. við fcrøcvitnum. við mæin-æiðum. við ráne. við raongum dome . . . / . . . við lygi við lafung . . . / . . . við

[64] laudancium Deum intercedite pro nobis miseris] *om.* L[12]

[65] Audientes autem haec . . . / . . . intercedite pro nobis miseris dicentes] Hoc audientes qui erant in penis, una voce exclamaverunt. Miserere Christe fili hominis C/spec

[66] L[4], L[12]

[67] vox Filii Dei] vox eius C/spec mss, vox L[4]

[68] L[12]

[69] Ego crucifixus sum pro vobis . . . / . . . ut viveretis mecum] Ego vero in mortem dedi me ipsum ut viveretis mecum L[12]

[70] M[5], P[6], P[8]

		wretches saying. O Jesus Christ, be merciful with the sons of men! Then hear their sound in the fourth heaven!'
34b *the voice of Christ I*	And then a voice from the Lord answers, thus speaking:	And the voice of the Son of God is heard by them through all pains saying: 'If you did not do good, wherefore do you ask me for a respite?
34c *the voice of Christ II*	'I was crucified for your sake and I was nailed with three nails. I was given vinegar to drink and endured scornful mistreatments and I was sold for a price. Then I endured slaughter and death for you so that you would be with me in eternal joy.	I was crucified for you, wounded with a spear, fastened with nails. You gave me vinegar to drink mixed with gall. I gave myself in martyrdom for you so you would live with me.
34d *the voice of Christ III*	And you responded with falsehood and lying, arrogance and homicide and cupidity and malice, false witness and spoken oaths, adultery and lust, laughter and mockery, overeating and excessive drinking, sloth and carnal lust, pride, swearing and cursing,	And you were liars in your life and thieves, greedy and envious, proud and slanderous, and you felt hatred for your neighbours and you neither gave the tithe nor honoured the holy Church of

Páls leizla. De visione Sancti Pauli

	ómiskunnsemi viðr þá er yðar þurftu. Þér fǫstuðuð illa minn píslardag ok helduð illa heilagt minn upprísudag ⟨ok⟩[48] hinn helga dróttinsdag.	Dei ecclesiam honorastis nec quidquam fecistis nec penitentiam nec elemosinam sed mendace in vita vestra fuistis et dolosi fuistis.[71][72]
34d/add *vox Christi III*	Ek léða yðr allt þat er þér þurftuð at hafa en þér villduð ekki **[149r]** gefa til minna þakka hvorki mat né drykk.[49] Óverðugr er sá at þiggja miskunnina seigir bókin er ǫngva vill ǫðrum veita.[50] Þá varð illr rytur í þeim vesǫlum sálum ok bádu en myskunnar.	
34g *Christus dat refrigerium*	Þá [svar]aði[51] Guðs rǫdd ok mælti. Fyrir mína mikla	Et ait Dominus. Propter Michaelem et Paulum et omnes angelos meos et maxime propter bonitatem meam et misericordiam[73] do vobis requiem ab hora nona sabbati usque ad horam primam ferie secunde.[74]

gaoldrum. við gerningum. við mykillæte NHB 87/23-30
[48] ⟨ok⟩ *om.* Tv, We
[49] en þér villduð ekki gefa til minna þakka hvorki mat né drykk] cf. *e.g.* hvat gerðu þer fyrir mic á veroldo fiðan ec þolda fva mykit fyrir yðr. Ec gaf yðr fol-skín. ok rægn. ok iarðar blóm. mat ok klæðe. lif ok hæilfu. en þér kunnuð mer ænga þoc NHB 34/25-28
[50] Óverðugr er sá at þiggja miskunnina seigir bókin er ǫngva vill ǫðrum veita] cf. þui so segir uorr herra at eg se ouerdugr at uera heyrdr.../... þui eg hefi þig so dyrt keypt med minni pinu er eg þolldi fyrir þig. og þar fyrir beidztu miskunnar. og þu skallt hafa miskunn. hann segir nei til þo þin miskunn uili þig⟨g⟩ia mig þa s(egir) þin rettuisi nei Æf 87/44-45; 48-51 (A)
[51] [svar]aði *foramen in cod.*

[71] Et vos mendaces .../... et dolosi fuistis] Sed vos fuistis furti avari invidi atque superbi et maledicti nec ullum bonum egistis nec penitenciam nec ieiunium nec elemosinam sed mendaces fuistis in vita vestra L[12]
[72] P[6], P[7], Br
[73] misericordiam] *om.* C/spec
[74] L[12]

(On) The Vision of Saint Paul

and lack of mercy to those who needed you. You fasted badly the day of my Passion and did not keep holy the day of my Ascension and the Holy day of the Lord.

God nor did you do penance or give alms, and rather you were liars and lived your lives with cunning.'

34d/add
the voice of Christ III

I granted you all that you needed to have but you were not willing to give me in thanks either food or drink. 'Unworthy to receive mercy is he,' says the book, 'who will not grant any to others.' And then there was an evil rowting among those wretched souls and they begged again for mercy.

34g
Christ gives a respite

Then the voice of God answered and said: 'Through

And the Lord said: 'Through Michael and Paul and all my angels and especially through my benevolence and mercy, I concede you a respite from the ninth hour of Saturday until the first hour of Monday.'

Páls leizla. De visione Sancti Pauli

miskunn ok bǿnn Michael engils ok Páls postola. Þá gef ek yðr hvíld frá nóni laugardagsins ok til fyrsto tíðar mánudags.

36
Benedicimus

Þá glǫddusk allar kristnir sálir við þá gjǫf en þǽr hinar vesligu sálir hrygðusk við þá gjǫf ok hvíld er ǫng[va][52] vonn áttu til Guðs. En mǽltu[53] kristnir sálir. Blezaðr sértu Guðs ⟨Sonr⟩[54] er þú gaft oss hvíld þessa. Er oss ok meiri hvíld at þessum helgum døgrum en at ǫllom dǫgum lífs vors.

Et laeti sunt qui crucibantur in inferno et clamaverunt dicentes. Benedicimus te Fili Dei[75] excelsi qui dignatus es nobis dare refrigerium in spacio unius diei et unius noctis. Plus valet nobis refrigerium unius diei quam omne tempus vite nostre super terram.[76][77]

37
Beati qui custodiunt diem dominicum

Nú mǽlir svá bókin af Guðs orðum. Sá er heldr vel hina helga dróttinsdag ok hinn helga píslardag Vors Herra Ihesu Christi ok gengr réttiliga til skrifta hann skal réttiliga með Guði vera utan enda.

Et qui custodierunt hunc sanctum diem habuerunt partem cum angelis Dei et vitam sempiternam.[78][79]

39a
Quot sunt pene?

Páll postoli spurði eingil hversu margar píslir[55] voru í helvíti.

Et interrogavit Paulus angelum[80] quot pene essent in inferno.[81]

39b
numerus penarum

Eingill svarar.[56] Þó at væri hundrað tungna ok væri ǫrtalin[57] þá vinnask þǽr eigi til

Cuis ait angelus. Sunt pene centum quadraginta tria mila. Et si essent centum viri

---

[52] aung[va] *foramen in cod.*
[53] mǽltu] mælti We
[54] Guðs ⟨Sonr⟩ *conieci* fili dei, *lect. dub.* Tv, [sonr?] We
[55] píslir] *inc.* B
[56] svarar] sagði B
[57] ǫrtalin] ǫrtali B

[75] Fili Dei] Fili David C/spec
[76] Plus valet nobis refrigerium ... / ... super terram] qui dedisti nobis refrigerium in spacio unius diei et duarum noccium super omne tempus vitae nostre C/spec
[77] L[12]
[78] et vitam sempiternam] *om.* C/spec
[79] L[12]
[80] angelum] *om.* C/spec
[81] L[12], L[4], P[6], P[7]

my great mercy and the prayers of Angel Michael and Apostle Paul, I give you a respite from the none of Saturday until the prime of Monday.'

36 *Bless thee*

Then all the Christian souls rejoiced over that gift and the wretched souls grieved at that gift and respite since they had no hope of God. And the Christian souls said: 'Blessed be thou, Son of God, for having granted us this respite. And we have more rest in these holy days than in all the days of our lives!'

And those who were tortured in Hell became joyful and cried out saying: 'Bless you, Son of the highest God, you deigned to concede us a consolation lasting one day and one night! For us a respite for one day is worth more than the entire time of our life on earth!'

37 *Blessed are those who keep the day of the Lord*

Now the book says this of the words of the Lord: 'The one who holds well the holy day of the Lord and the holy day of the Passion of Christ and goes properly to confession, he shall justly be with God without end.'

And those who kept this day holy have had share with the angels of God and eternal life.

39a *How many are the pains?*

The apostle Paul asked the angel how many tortures there were in Hell.

And Paul asked the angel how many pains are in Hell.

39b *number of the pains*

The angel answers: 'If there were one hundred tongues and they were quick of speech, they will not be able

To this the angel said: 'The pains are one thousand four hundred and three. And if there were one hundred

28 Páls leizla. De visione Sancti Pauli

at telja allar píslir er í helvíte eru.[58]

loquentes ab inicio mundi et unusquisque centum linguas ferreas haberet non possent[82] dinumerare[83] penas inferni.[84]

39b/add
numerus penarum

Ok þér sǫmu tungur væri[59] fyrr mǿddar máðar ok móðar en fengi talt alla þá hluti gǿzku ok sælu er með Guði eru í himnum ok hans helgum mǫnnum.

41
Audientes convertamur

Nú hǫfum vér heyrt hversu mikit skilr eilífa sælu ok eilífa kval gǫrum sem David segir í Psalterium.[60] *Declina a malo*[61] *et fac bonum.* Látum af íllu ok gǿrum[62] gótt.[63] Þá eigum vér vist hjá Kristi ok erum þá við skildir þessar[64] píslir[65] sem nú hefir verit frá[66] sagt ok

Nos igitur fratres karissimi tanta mala[85] audientes convertamus ad Dominum Ihesum Christum qui nos amantissime redemit per suum sacrum sanguinem ut regnamus cum ipso in secula seculorum. Amen.[86]

---

[58] þó at væri hundrað tungna ok væri ǫrtalin. Þá vinnask þær eigi til at telja allar píslir er í helvíte eru] cf. þoat c tungna uæri þar j hueriu hofdi þa mundi eigi geta up talt *fatt er þat sem hann sagdi oss DL 74/14-15 (AM 681a)

[59] *post* væri *add.* en *B*

[60] psallterium] psaltarnum Tv, We

[61] malo] male *B*

[62] gjǫrum] gjǫr *B*

[63] Declina a malo et fac bonum. Látum af íllu ok gjǫrum gótt] Ps. 36:27

[64] þessar] þessum *B ante* þessum *add.* frá *B*

[65] píslir] píslum *B*

[66] frá *om. B*

---

[82] *post* possent *add.* enarrare nec C/spec

[83] *post* dinumerare *add.* minores/peiores C/spec

[84] L[12], L[4], P[6], P[7]

[85] tanta mala] ista mala C/spec mss

[86] L[12], M[5], P[8]

	to count all the pains that are in Hell.	men talking from the beginning of the world and each of them had one hundred tongues of iron, they would not be able to count the pains of Hell.'
39b/add *number of the pains*	And before they could count all those things of grace and bliss that are in heaven with God and His holy men, those same tongues would be torn, worn out and exhausted.'	
41 *Hearing this we convert*	Now that we have heard how much separates eternal bliss from eternal torment, let us do as David says in the Psalter: '*Decline from evil and do good, forsake evil and do good.*' Then we can dwell with Christ and are thus separated from the pains which have been related here.	Therefore, dearest brothers, after hearing so much evil, let us turn towards the Lord, Jesus Christ, who redeemed us through His blood, so that we reign with Him throughout endless ages. Amen.

sá er ǽ sǽll er þar skal blífa ok vera.

41/add
Audientes convertamur

Nú gerum af því þorf vorra ok nauðsýn ok látum eigi ganga á oss órøkt ok hirtunarleysi sem[67] flesta menn tælir. Þá hina litlu stund er vér erum hér í heimi. Nú eigum vér svá at gera sem vér viljum þessa hina litlu stund at vér séum utan enda sælir með Guði. Þat vill hann ok hans helgir menn. Per omnia secula seculorum. Amen.

---

[67] sem] en *B*

And he is forever blessed,
the one who shall remain
and be there.

41/add
Hearing this we convert

Now let us fulfil our obligations and necessities and let not illegitimacy and the want of punishment overtake us, as happens to many men during this little while in which we are here in this world. Now we must do that which we want in this little while, so that we may be blessed with God without end. That is what He and His holy men wish. Throughout endless ages. Amen.

BIBLIOGRAPHY AND ABBREVIATIONS

Abbreviations

BHH = Teresi, Loredana, ed., 2003. '*Be Heofonwarum 7 be Helwarum*: A Complete Edition'.
BL = British Library.
BnF = Bibliothèque nationale de France.
CCCM = *Corpus Christianorum, Continuatio Mediaevalis*. Turnhout, 1966–.
CCSL = *Corpus Christianorum, Series Latina*. Turnhout, 1954–.
DI = Jón Sigurðsson et al., eds, 1857–1976. *Diplomatarium Islandicum. Íslenzkt fornbréfasafn*.
DLe = Cahill, Peter, ed., 1983. *Duggals leiðsla*. Reykjavík.
DN = *Diplomatarium Norvegicum. Oldbreve til kundskab om Norges indre og ydre forhold, sprog, slægter, sæder, lovgivning og rettergang i middelalderen* 1847–1995. Christiania.
HMS = Unger, Carl R., ed., 1877. *Heilagra manna sögur*. Oslo.
IHB = de Leeuw van Weenen, Andrea, ed., 2003. *The Icelandic Homily Book*. Reykjavík.
NGL = Keyser, Rudolf and Peter A. Munch, eds, 1846–95. *Norges gamle Love indtil 1387*. 5 vols. Christiania.
NHB = Indrebø, Gustav, ed. 1931. *Gamal norsk Homiliebok. Cod AM 619 4to*. Oslo.
ONP = *Ordbog over det norrøne prosasprog* 1989. Copenhagen.
PL = *Patrologiae Cursus Completus, Series Latina* 1844–65. Ed. Jacques-Paul Migne et al. Paris.
PLe = *Páls leizla*.
PS = Unger, Carl R., ed., 1874. *Postola sögur*. Christiania.
VT = *Visio Tnugdali*.
Æf = Einar G. Pétursson, ed., 1976. *Miðaldaævintýri þydd úr ensku*. Reykjavík.

Bibliography

Abram, Christopher 2007. 'Anglo-Saxon Homilies in their Scandinavian Context'. In Aaron J. Kleist, ed., *The Old English Homily. Precedent, Practice, Appropriation*. Studies in the Early Middle Ages 17. Turnhout, 425–44.
Abram, Christopher 2014. 'Anglo-Saxon Influence in the Old Norwegian Homily Book'. *Mediaeval Scandinavia* 14, 1–35.
Akehurst, F. R. P., trans. and intr., 1996. *The Etablissements de Saint Louis. Thirteenth-Century Law Texts from Tours, Orléans, and Paris*. Philadelphia.
Ambrosius Autpertus 1979. *Sermo in purificatione sanctae Mariae*. In *Ambrosii Autperti opera*. Ed. Robert Weber. *CCCM* XXVII B. Turnhout, 975–1102.
Andersson, Aron 1949. *English Influence in Norwegian and Swedish Figurescuplture in Wood 1220–70*. Stockholm.
Augustinus de Dacia 1929. *Rotolus pugillaris* = 'Rotulus pugillaris examinatus atque editus'. Ed. Angelus Walz. *Angelicum* 6, 245–78 and 548–71.

Baika, Gabriella Ildiko 2007. *Lingua indisciplinata. A Study of Transgressive Speech in the 'Romance of the Rose' and the 'Divine Comedy'*. Unpublished PhD dissertation. Pittsburg.

Beda Venerabilis 1955. *Homilia* 18 *In purificatione s. Mariae*. In *Bedae Venerabilis Opera*, Pars III: *Opera homiletica*. Ed. David Hurst, *CCSL* 122. Turnhout, 128–33.

Bekker-Nielsen, Hans 1960. 'Den gammelnorske paaskeprædiken og Gregor den Store'. *Maal og Minne*, 99–104.

Berg, Kirsten M. 2010. 'Homilieboka – for hvem og til hva?' In *Vår eldste bok. Skrift, miljø og biletbruk i den norske homilieboka*. Ed. Odd Einar Haugen and Åslaug Ommundsen. Bibliotheca Nordica 3l. Osl, 35–77.

Blanton, Thomas B. IV 2007. *Constructing a New Covenant. Discursive Strategies in the Damascus Document and Second Corinthians*. Wissenschaftliche Untersuchungen zum Neuen Testament 2. Reihe. Tübingen.

Blount, Brian K. 2009. *Revelation: A Commentary*. The New Testament Library. Louisville.

Boitani, Piero and Torti, Anna, eds., 1999. *The Body and the Soul in Medieval Literature*. Cambridge.

Bullitta, Dario 2017a. 'Sources, Context, and English Provenance of the Old Danish *Visio Pauli*'. *Journal of English and Germanic Philology* 116 (1).

Bullitta, Dario 2017b. *Niðrstgningar saga: Sources, Transmission, and Theology of the Old Norse Descent into Hell*. Toronto Old Norse-Icelandic Series 11. Toronto.

Bullitta, Dario 2014. '*Crux Christi muscipula fuit diabolo*: Un sermone agostiniano dietro la cattura di Satana nella *Niðrstgningar saga*'. In Carla Falluomini, ed., *Intorno alle saghe norrene. XIV Seminario Avanzato in Filologia Germanica*. Alessandria, 129–54.

Bultot, Robert 1964. 'Les *Meditationes* Pseudo-Bernardines sur la connaissance de la condition humaine. Problèmes d'histoire littéraire'. *Sacris Erudiri: Jaarboek voor Godsdienstwetenschappen* 15, 256–92.

Cahill, Peter, ed., 1983. *Duggals leiðsla*. Reykjavík. [DLe].

Cameron, Alan 1967. 'The Virgilian Cliché of the Hundred Mouths in Corippus'. *Philologus*, 308–09.

Casey, Robert P. 1933. 'The Apocalypse of Paul'. *Journal of Theological Studies* 34, 1–32.

Ciccarese, Maria Pia, ed., 1987. *Visioni dell'aldilí in occidente. Fonti, modelli, testi*. Biblioteca Patristica 8. Florence.

Collings, Lucy Grace 1969. *The Codex Scardensis: Studies in Icelandic Hagiography*. Unpublished PhD dissertation. Ithaca: Cornell University.

Conti, Aidan 2008. 'The Old Norse Afterlife of Ralph d'Escures's *Homilia de assumptione Mariae*'. *Journal of English and Germanic Philology* 107, 215–38.

Courcelle, Pierre 1955. 'Histoire du cliché virgilien des cent bouches'. *Revue des études latines* 33, 231–40.

Dinzelbacher, Peter 1973. *Die Jenseitsbrücke im Mittelalter*. Dissertationen der Universität Wien 104. Vienna.

Diplomatarium Norvegicum. *Oldbreve til kundskab om Norges indre og ydre forhold, sprog, slægter, sæder, lovgivning og rettergang i middelalderen 1847–1995*. Christiania.

Dondaine, Antoine 1948. 'Guillaume Peyraut, vie et oeuvres'. *Archivium Fratrum Praedicatorum* 18, 162–236.

Durandus 1859. *Rationale divinorum officiorum = Rationale divinorum officiorum a rev.mo domino Guilelmo Durando*. Ed. Vincenzo d'Avino. Naples.

Einar G. Pétursson, ed., 1976. *Miðaldaævintýri þydd úr ensku*. Reykjavík. [*Æf*].

Foote, Peter G. 1959. *The Pseudo-Turpin Chronicle in Iceland: A Contribution to the Study of Karlamagnús saga*. London Mediæval Studies Monograph No. 4. London.

Fowler, David C. and John Spencer Hill 1992. 'Harp'. In David L. Jeffrey, ed., *A Dictionary of Biblical Tradition in English Literature*. Grand Rapids, 330–32.

Garland, David E. 1999. *2 Corinthians. An Exegetical and Theological Exposition of Holy Scripture*. The New American Commentary 29. Nashville, 1999.

Gering, Hugo, ed. 1882–84. *Islendzk Æventyri: Isländische Legenden, Novellen und Märchen*, 1. Halle.

Gougaud, Louis 1927. 'La croyance au répit périodique des damnés dans les légendes irlandaises'. In *Mélanges bretons et celtiques offerts í M. J. Loth* Paris and Rennes, 63–72.

Gregorius Magnus 2006. *Dialogi* = Manlio Simonetti, ed. and trans. *Gregorio Magno, Storie di santi e di diavoli (Dialoghi)*, 2, comm. Salvatore Pricoco, Scrittori greci e latini. Fondazione Lorenzo Valla. Milan, 280/52–285/2.

Guillelmus Alvernus 2011. *Sermo* 166 (*in uigilia paschatis*. In Franco Morenzoni, ed., *Sermones de tempore*, CXXXVI–CCCXXIII. *CCCM* 230A. Turnhout, 132/1–134/74.

Heggstad, Leiv, Finn Hødnebø and Erik Simensen 1975. *Nørron ordbok*. 3rd edition. Oslo.

Henningham, Eleanor Kellogg 1939. *An Early Latin Debate of the Body and Soul. Preserved in MS Royal A III in the British Museum*. Unpublished PhD dissertation. New York University.

Indrebø, Gustav, ed. 1931. *Gamal norsk Homiliebok. Cod AM 619 4to*. Norsk historisk kjeldeskrift-institutt, Skrifter 54. Oslo [*NHB*].

Iohannes de Caulibus 1997. *Meditaciones vitae Christi olim S. Bonauenturo attributae*. Ed. Mary Stallings-Taney. *CCCM* 153. Turnhout, 1997.

Jacoby, Joachim 2005. 'The Image of Pity in the Later Middle Ages. Images, Prayers and Prayer instructions'. *Studi medievali* 46 (2), 560–605.

James, Montague R., trans., 1924. *The Apocryphal New Testament*. Oxford.

Jiroušková, Lenka 2006. *Die Visio Pauli. Wege und Wandlungen einer orien-talischen Apokryphe im lateinischen Mittelalter unter Einschluss der alttschechischen und deutschsprachigen Textzeugen*. Mittellateinische Studien und Texte 34. Leiden and Boston, 2006.

Johnsson, David F. 1993. 'The Five Horrors of Hell: An Insular Homiletic Motif'. *English Studies* 74, 414–31.

Jón Sigurðsson et al., eds, 1857–1976. *Diplomatarium Islandicum. Íslenzkt fornbréfasafn*, Copenhagen and Reykjavík. [DI].

Jorgensen, Peter A., ed., 1997. *The Story of Jonatas in Iceland* Reykjavík.

Kålund, Kristian, ed., 1883. *Fljótsdœla hin meiri, eller, Den længere Droplaugarsona-saga*. Samfund til udgivelse af gammel nordisk litteratur 11. Copenhagen.

Kålund, Kristian 1889–94. *Katalog over Den Arnamagnæanske Håndskriftsamling* 2. Copenhagen.

Kålund, Kristian, ed., 1918. *Alfrœði íslenzk. Islandsk encyklopædisk litteratur* 3. Samfund til udgivelse af gammel nordisk litteratur 45. Copenhagen.

Kabir, Ananya Jahanara 2001. *Paradise, Death and Doomsday in Anglo-Saxon Literature*. Cambridge Studies in Anglo-Saxon England 32. Cambridge.

Kamerick, Kathleen 2002. *Popular Piety and Art in the Late Middle Ages: Image Worship and Idolatry in England 1350–1500*. New York.

von Karajan, Theodor G., ed., 1846. *Deutsche Sprach-Denkmale des zwölften Jahrhunderts*. Vienna.

Keefer, Sarah Larratt 2009. '*Ðonne se cirlisca man ordales weddigeð*: The Anglo-Saxon Lay Ordeal'. In Stephen Baxter, Catherine E. Karkov and David Pelteret, eds, *Early Medieval Studies in Memory of Patrick Wormald*. Farnahm and Burlington, 355–57.

Ker, Neil R. 1969. *Medieval Manuscripts in British Libraries* 1: *London*. Oxford.

Keyser, Rudolf and Peter A. Munch, eds, 1846–95. *Norges gamle Love indtil 1387*. 5 vols. Christiania.[*NGL*]

Kirby, Ian J. 1980. *Biblical Quotations in Old Icelandic–Norwegian Religious Literature* 2: *Introduction*. Reykjavík.

de Leeuw van Weenen, Andrea, ed., 2003. *The Icelandic Homily Book. Perg 15 4to in the Royal Library, Stockholm*. Íslensk handrit/Icelandic manuscripts, Series in quarto 3. Reykjavík. [*IHB*].

L'Estrange Ewen, Cecil 1929 repr. 2011. *Witch Hunting and Witch Trials: The Indictments for Witchcraft from the Records of 1373 Assizes Held for the Home Circuit AD 1559–1736*. London.

Leroquais, Victor 1927. *Les livres d'heures manuscrits de la Bibliotheque nationale* 1. Paris.

Líndal, Sigurður, ed., 1974. *Saga Íslands* 5. Reykjavík.

Loewenstein, David 2013. *Treacherous Faith: The Specter of Heresy in Early Modern English Literature*. Oxford.

Loth, Agnete, ed., 1969. *Reykjahólabók: Islandske helgenlegender*. Editiones Arnamagnæanæ A 15–16. Copenhagen.

Lucas Tudensis 2009. *De altera uita*. Ed. Emma Falque Rey. *CCCM* 74A.Turnhout.

McDougall, David 1983. *Studies in Prose Style of the Old Icelandic and Old Norwegian Homily Books*.Unpublished PhD dissertation. University College London.

McDougall, David 1993. 'Homilies (West Norse)'. In Phillip Pulsiano, Kirsten Wolf et al., eds. *Medieval Scandinavia*: *An Encyclopedia*. Garland Encyclopedias of the Middle Ages 1. New York, 290–92.

Marchand, James, ed., 1976. 'The Old Icelandic *Joca Monachorum*', *Medieval Scandinavia* 9, 99–126.

Margerøy, Hallvard 1985. '*In dedicatione ecclesiæ sermo*. Om overleveringa av Stavkyrkjepreika'. *Opuscula* 8, 96–122.

Meier, Esther 2006. *Die Gregorsmesse: Funktionen eines spätmittelalterlichen Bildtypus*. Cologne, Weimar and Vienna.

Mertens, Volker 1975. 'Die frühmhd. *Visio Pauli*. Untersuchungen zur Quellenfrage'. In Peter Kesting, ed., *Würzburger Prosastudien* 2. Medium Aevum Philologische Studien 31. Munich, 77–92.

Moe, Moltke 1927. 'Middelalderens visionsdigtning'. In Knut Liestøl, ed., *Moltke Moes samlede skrifter* 3. Instituttet for sammenlignede kulturforskning, ser. B, 1, 6, 9. Oslo, 199–247.

Moeller, Eugène, Jean-Marie Clément and Bertrand Coppieters 't Wallant, eds, 1993. *Corpus orationum* 3, D pars altera, *Orationes 1708–2389*. CCSL 160 B. Turnhout.

Myers, A. R. and David C. Douglas, eds, 1969. *English Historical Documents* 4, *1327–1485*. London.

Nicol, Donald M. 1998. *Byzantium and Venice. A Study in Diplomatic and Cultural Relations*. Cambridge.

Oliver, Lisi 2001. *The Body Legal in Barbarian Law*. Toronto Anglo-Saxon Series 9. Toronto.

Ordbog over det norrøne prosasprog / A Dictionary of Old Norse Prose. Registre / Indices. 1989. Copenhagen. [*ONP*].

Páll Eggert Ólason, Jón Guðnason and Ólafur Þ. Kristjánsson, eds, 1951. *Íslenzkar æviskrár frá landnámstímum til ársloka 1940* 4. Reykjavík.

Parrot, Douglas M., ed., 1996. 'The Apocalypse of Paul (V,*2*)'. Intr. and trans. George W. MacRae and William R. Murdock. In James M. Robinson, ed., *Nag Hammadi Library in English. The Definitive New Translation of the Gnostic Scriptures, Complete in One Volume*. Leiden. 4th ed., rev. Richard Smith, 255–59.

Patrologiae Cursus Completus, *Series Latina* 1844–65. Ed. Jacques-Paul Migne et al. Paris. [PL].

Pinkerton, John 1809. *A General Collection of the Best and Most Interesting Voyages and Travels in all Parts of the World Many of Which are Now Translated into English Digested on a New Plan* 3. London.

Pseudo-Bernardus Claraeuallensis. *Meditationes piissimae de cognitione humanae conditionis*. PL 184, cols 485–508.

Raimundus Lullus 2001. *Liber de homine* (*op. 94*) [*translatio latina e textu catalano Lulli ipsius iussu confecta*]. In *Opera latina XXI* (*92–96*). Ed. Fernando Dominguez Reboiras. CCCM 112. Turnhout, 152–301.

Roberts, Alexander and James Donaldson 1870. *Ante-Nicene Christian Library: Translations of the Writings of the Fathers down to A.D. 325*. 16: *Apocryphal Gospels, Acts, and Revelations*. Trans. Alexander Walker. Edinburgh, 477–92.

Rosenstiehl, Jean-Marc 1990. 'L'itinéraire de Paul dans l'au-delà: Contribution à l'étude de l'Apocalypse apocryphe de Paul'. In Peter Nagel, ed., *Carl-Schmidt-Kolloquium an der Martin-Luther-Universität Halle-Wittenberg*, Wissenschaftliche Beiträge 23 K 9. Halle-Wittenberg, 199–207.

Bibliography

Ruff, Julius R. 2001. *Early Modern Europe 1500–1800*. Cambridge.
van Ruiten, Jacques T. A. G. M. V. 2003. 'The Four Rivers of Eden in the *Apocalypse of Paul (Visio Pauli)*: The Intertextual Relationship of Gen 2:10–14 and the *Apocalypse of Paul* 23'. In F. García Martínez and G. P. Luttikhuizen, eds, *Jerusalem, Alexandria, Rome: Studies in Ancient Cultural Interaction in Honour of A. Hilhorst*. Leiden, 263–84.
Schwerhoff, Gerd 2005. *Zungen wie Schwerter: Blasphemie in alteuropäischen Gesellschaften 1200–1650*. Konstanz.
Silverstein, Theodore, ed., 1935. *Visio Sancti Pauli, The History of the Apocalypse in Latin together with nine Texts*. Studies and Documents 4. London.
Silverstein, Theodore 1962. 'The Date of the Apocalypse of Paul'. *Mediaeval Studies* 24, 335–48.
Stefán Karlsson, ed., 1963. *Islandske originaldiplomer indtil 1450: Tekst*. Editiones Arnamagnæanæ Series A 7. Copenhagen.
Stein-Wilkeshuis, Martine 1991. 'Punishment in Iceland. A Survey'. In *La peine. Punishment. 2 : Europe avant le XIIIe siècle. Europe before the 18th Century*. Recuils de la société Jean Bodin pour l'histoire comparative des institutions. Transactions of the Jean Bodin Society for Comparative Institutional History 56 Brussels, 87–102.
Storm, Gustav, ed. and trans., 1896. 'En gammel Gildeskraa fra Trondhjem'. In *Sproglig-historiske Studier tilegnede Prof. C. R. Unger*. Oslo, 217–26.
Teresi, Loredana, ed., 2003. '*Be Heofonwarum* ⁊ *be Helwarum*: A Complete Edition'. In *Early Medieval English Texts and Interpretations: Studies Presented to Donald G. Scragg*. Ed. Elaine Treharne and Susan Rosser. Medieval and Renaissance Texts and Studies 252. Tempe.
Turville-Petre, Gabriel 1972. 'The Old Norse Homily on the Dedication'. In *Nine Norse Studies*. Viking Society for Northern Research Text Series 5. London, 79–101.
Tveitane, Mattias 1963. '*Visio Pauli* og den norrøne *Michaels saga*'. *Maal og Minne*, 106–11.
Tveitane, Mattias, ed., 1965. *En norrøn versjon av Visio Pauli*. Årbok for universitetet i Bergen. Humanistisk serie 1964 no. 3. Oslo.
Unger, Carl R., ed., 1871. *Mariu saga: Legender om jomfru Maria og hendes jertegn* 1. Oslo.
Unger, Carl R., ed., 1874. *Postola sögur. Legendariske fortællinger om apostlernes liv, deres kamp for kristendommens udbredelse samt deres martyrdød*. Christiania. [*PS*].
Unger, Carl R., ed., *Páls saga postola* II. In *PS*, 263/19–279/22.
Unger, Carl R., ed., 1877. *Heilagra manna sögur. Fortællinger og legender om hellige mænd og kvinder*. Oslo. [*HMS*].
Unger, Carl R., ed., *Mikjáls saga*. In *HMS* 1, 676–713.
Veturliði Óskarsson 2009. 'Um sögnina *blífa*, vöxt hennar og viðgang í íslensku'. *Íslenskt mál og almenn málfræði* 31, 189–224.
Weber, Robert et al., eds, 2007. *Biblia sacra iuxta Vulgatam versionem*. 5th ed., rev. Roger Gryson. Stuttgart.

Wellendorf, Jonas 2009. *Kristeleg visionslitteratur i norrøn tradition*. Bibliotheca Nordica 2. Oslo.
Widding, Ole and Hans Bekker-Nielsen 1959. 'A Debate of the Body and Soul in Old Norse Literature'. *Mediaeval Studies* 21, 272–89.
Willard, Rudolph 1935. 'Address of the Soul to the Body', *Publications of the Modern Language Association* 50: 4, 957–83.
Wirth, Karl-August 1953. *Die Entstehung der Drei-Nagel-Cruzifixus. Seine typengeschichtliche Entwicklung in Frankreich und Deutschland bis zur Mitte des 13. Jahrhunderts*. Unpublished PhD Dissertation. Frankfurt: Goethe-Universität.
Wirth, Karl-August 1958 'Dreinagelkruzifixus', in *Reallexikon der deutschen Kunstgeschichte*, vol. 4. Stuttgart, 524–25.
Wolf, Kirsten 2001. 'Gregory's Influence on Old Norse–Icelandic Religious Literature'. In Rolf H. Bremmer Jr, Kees Dekker and David F. Johnson, eds, *Rome in the North: The Early Reception of Gregory in Germanic Europe*. Mediaevalia Groningana New Series 4. Paris, Leuven and Sterling, 255–75.
Wright, Charles D., 1993. *The Irish Tradition in Old English Literature*. Cambridge Studies in Anglo-Saxon England 8. Cambridge.
Þorvaldur Bjarnarson, ed., 1878. *Leifar fornra kristinna fræða íslenzkra. Codex Arna-Magnæanus 677 4to auk annara enna elztu brota af íslenzkum guðfræðisritum*. Copenhagen.

INDEX OF SCRIPTURAL QUOTATIONS

Genesis 2:10–14, vii n14
Matthew 27:26, xxxvi
Matthew 27:29, xxxvii
Matthew 27:35, xxxvi
Mark 15:17, xxxvii
Mark 16:1–5, x
Luke 1:28–38, xxvii
Luke 2:21, xxxv
Luke 22:44, xxxv
John 19:2, xxxvii
John 19:5, xxxvii
John 19:34, xxxvi
2 Corinthians 11:24–31, xxxi
2 Corinthians 12:1, v n1
2 Corinthians 12:2–4, v
2 Corinthians 12:2–6, xxxi
2 Corinthians 12:5, v n1
2 Corinthians 12:7, v n2
James 2:13, xli n165
Revelation 7:4, xxvi n115
Revelation 14:1, xxvi n115
Revelation 19:12, xxxvii

Páls leizla

INDEX OF MANUSCRIPTS

Brno
  Státní Vědecká Knihovna, Mk 99 [I. 29] (Br), xiii n43

Cambridge
  Corpus Christi College, 302, xxviii n123
  Saint John's College, Ms. D.20 (95) (C[6]), xiv n43
  University Library, Harley 7333, xlv n170
  University Library, Kk.i.6, xlv n170

Copenhagen
  Den Arnamagnæanske Samling, AM 234 fol., xxxv
  Den Arnamagnæanske Samling, AM 58 4to, xxiii n92
  Den Arnamagnæanske Samling, AM 60 4to, xxiii n90
  Den Arnamagnæanske Samling, AM 619 4to (NHB), x n28
  Den Arnamagnæanske Samling, AM 657 a–b 4to, ix n23
  Den Arnamagnæanske Samling, AM 681 a 4to, ix n23, xxvii n118, xxviii,
  Den Arnamagnæanske Samling, AM 681 b 4to, ix n23
  Den Arnamagnæanske Samling, AM 681 c 4to, ix, ix n23, xi, xii, xxvi, xliv
  Den Arnamagnæanske Samling, AM 683 c 4to, xxxviii n158
  Den Arnamagnæanske Samling, AM 683 d 4to, xxxviii, xl
  Den Arnamagnæanske Samling, AM 31 8vo, xxiii n91
  Det Kongelige Bibliotek, GKS 1155 a fol., xxiii n93
  Det Kongelige Bibliotek, Kall 616 4to, xxiii n96

Dublin
  Trinity College, TCD 277 (D[2]), xxiv n43
  Trinity College, TDC 519 (D[3]), xxiv n125

Leipzig
  Universitätsbibliothek (Bibliotheca Albertina) 1608 (Le), viii n18

London
  BL, Additional 9066, xlv n170
  BL, Cotton Faustina A.IX, xxviii n123
  BL, Harleian 2851 (L[4]), xiii n43
  BL, Royal 11.B.III (L[9]), xiii n43, xxix n125
  St Paul's Cathedral Library, Ms. 8 (L[12]), xiii n43

Munich
  Bayerische Staatsbibliothek, clm 14348 (M[5]), xiii n43

Oslo
  Norsk Riksarkivet, 50 c, xii n83

Oxford
  Merton College, Ms 13 (O[5]), xxix n125

Index 41

Padua
  Biblioteca Antoniana, 473, Scaff. XXI, ff. 147v–149r (Pa), xxix n25
Paris
  BnF, lat. 3528 (P^6), xiv n43
  BnF, lat. 3529A (P^7), xiii n43
  BnF, lat. 5266 (P^8), xiii n43, xix n125
  BnF, nouv. acq. lat. 1631, vii n11
Reykjavík
  Landsbókasafn Íslands – Háskólabókasafn, JS 43 4to, x n26
  Stofnun Árna Magnússonar í íslenskum fræðum, AM 347 fol. (Belgdalsbók), xxii n84
  Stofnun Árna Magnússonar í íslenskum fræðum, AM 350 fol. (Skarðsbók or Codex Scardensis), xxii n85
  Stofnun Árna Magnússonar í íslenskum fræðum, AM 238 4to, xxiii n99
  Stofnun Árna Magnússonar í íslenskum fræðum, AM 279 a 4to (Þingeyrarbók), xi n33
  Stofnun Árna Magnússonar í íslenskum fræðum, AM 624 4to, ix, ix n24, x n26, xi, xii, xxvi, xli, xliv, xlv, xlvii, xlviii
Sankt Gallen
  Stiftsbibliothek, 682 (StG^1), viii n18
  Stadtbibliothek (Vadianische Bibliothek), 317 (StG^L), xviii n70
Schlägl
  Prämonstratenser-Stiftsbibliothek, Cpl. 226 (Sch), xiii n43
Stockholm
  Kungliga Biblioteket, Cod. Holm Perg. 3 fol (Reykjahólabók), xxiii n95
  Kungliga Biblioteket, Cod. Holm. Perg. 15 4to (*IHB*), x n29
Uppsala
  Universitetsbiblioteket, C 22 (U^1), viii n20
  Universitetsbiblioteket, C 77 (U^2), viii n21
  Universitetsbiblioteket, C 212 (U^3), viii n21
Vatican City
  Biblioteca Apostolica Vaticana, Pal. lat. 216 (V^2), viii n18
  Biblioteca Apostolica Vaticana, Pal. lat. 220 (V^3), viii n18
Vienna
  Österreichische Nationalbibliothek, Ser. Nova 388, xxxiii

GENERAL INDEX

Abram, patriarch (7th c. BC), xxviii, xliv
Adam, Bishop of Melrose (ǫ 1222), xx n78
af einum rikum manni, exemplum 29 of the Æfintýr collection, xli
Albigensian heresy, xxxvi
Ambrosius Autpertus, Frankish Abbot of San Vincenzo al Volturno († 784), xxxv n145
Amos, minor prophet (8th c. BC), vii n13
Andsvar Norðlendinga um presta og kirkna skyldur, xlv, xlv
angel(s)
    ——, a great army of, xli n163
    ——, a multitude of, vii
    ——, unidentified, vi, xxxiii, xxxiv
Anglo-Saxon
    ——, homilists, xli
    ——, text, xxviii
Apocalypse *see* Doomsday
Apocalypse of Paul
    ——, Coptic, vi
    ——, Greek see *Apocalypsis Pauli*
Apocalypsis Pauli
    ——, Greek, first redaction, vi
    ——, Greek, second redaction, vi
    ——, Latin, Heaven-Hell redaction, vi, vii, viii
    ——, Latin, Hell redaction, *see Visio Pauli*
Augustine of Dacia, prior of Dacia, Denmark († 1282), xxxii
Austin Friars, xv

Baldwin II Porphyrogenitus, Emperor of Constantinople († 1273), xxxvii n155
Be heofonwarum and be helwarum, Anglo-Saxon homily (*BHH*), xxviii, xxix, xliv
Bede, doctor of the Church in Monkwearmouth-Jarrow († 735), xi n32, xxv n145
Bergr Sokkason, Abbot of Munkaþverá († *c.*1370), xxx, xxxii, xxxiv
Bernard of Clairvaux, doctor of the Church († 1153), ix
Bible
    ——, Douay-Rheims, v n1, xlix
    ——, Vulgate, v n1
Bjarni Ólason, a farmer at Hvassafell, Iceland (15th c.), xlvi
blífa ok vera, xi, xxiii, xlv
Book of Hours, xxxix
Borgarþingslǫg, *see* laws
British Isles, viii
Brother Robert of Norway, Norwegian cleric (13th c.), x n26, xxi

Caithness, Scotland
    ——, farmers of, xx n78

Campania, Italy, vi n10
Carolingian
———, manuscripts, viii
Christ
———, abuses, xxxviii, xlii
———, *arma Christi*, xxxviii
———, blood, xxxv, xxxviii, xlii
———, bound in fetters, xxxiv
———, bright as the sun, xli n163
———, *Christus victor*, xli
———, circumcision, xxxv, xxxviii n157
———, City of, vii,
———, crown of thorns, xxxvii, xxxviii, xxxix
———, crucifixion, xxx, xxxiv, xxxv, xxxvii, xxxviii, xliv
———, defeat over Satan, xli n163
———, descending from heaven, vii
———, feet, xxxv, xxxvi, xxxvii
———, five holy wounds, xxxv, xxxviii, xxxix
———, hammer, xxxviii
———, Holy Grail, xxxviii
———, holy lance, xxxv, xxxviii
———, holy sponge, xxxviii
———, innocent Lamb, xxxix
———, instruments of the Passion, *see arma Christi*
    , King of kings see *Christus victor*
———, kingly crown, xxxviii n156, xli n163
———, lamentations, xiv, xli
———, the Lord, vii, xxvi, xxxiv
———, the man in, *see* Paul of Tarsus
———, the Man of Sorrow, *see Vir dolorum*
———, as a mangled child, xlii, xliii
———, mercy, xli, xlii, xliii, xlv
———, the Messiah, xvi
———, mildness, xxx
———, on the altar, vii, xxxix
———, the Passion of, xxxvi, xxxvii, xxxviii, xxxix, xlii, xliii, xlv
———, the pierced side of, xxxv, xxxvi, xlii
———, reed sceptre, xxxviii
———, reproaching speech to humanity, xxxiv
———, the Resurrection of, xviii
———, riding a white horse, xli n163
———, righteousness, xlii
———, sacrificed, xxxvii, xxxix
———, scourged, xxxvi
———, sovereign ruler, *see Christus victor*

———, suffering, xxxix, xlii, xliii, xlv
———, sweat of, xxxv
———, three-tongued scourge, xxxviii
———, the Trinity, xviii, xxx
———, vinegar and gall, xxxix
———, *Vir dolorum*, xxxviii, xli
———, visions of, *see* Christophanies
———, voice of, xxxiv
———, warrior-king, see *Christus victor*
Christian
——— communities, v, vi
——— literature, v
Christian I, King of Norway and Denmark († 1481), xlvi
Christophanies, v
Church
———, Eastern, vi
confessors
———, Dominican, xix, xxxii
———, handbook for, xix, xliv
Constantinople, vi, xxxvii
Copenhagen, Denmark, xlvii
the Creation, xxvii, xxxi
the cross
———, agonies on, xxxii, xxxvii
———, arms of, xxxv
———, four nails of, xxxv, xxxvi, xxxvii
———, hidden divinity of, xli n163
———, Hours of the, xxxix
———, lower part of, xxxv
———, three nails of, xxx, xxxv, xxxvi, xxxvii, xxxviii, xlv
crucifix(es)
———, Balke, Norway, xxxviii n156
———, Bellinge, Denmark, xxxviii n156
———, Bergen, Norway, xxxviii n156
———, collapsed body, xxxvii
———, crown of thorns, xxxvii, xxxviii, xxxviii n156, xxxviii n157, xxxix
———, Elverum, Norway, xxxviii
———, four-nails, xxxvii
———, Fresvik, Norway, xxxviii n156
———, Fåberg, Norway, xxxviii n156
———, Hamre, Norway, xxxviii n156
———, Hedal, Norway, xxxviii n156
———, Heggen, Norway, xxxviii n156
———, Hølandet, Norway, xxxviii n156
———, Kjose, Norway, xxxviii n156

―――, Mofalla, Sweden, xxxviii n156
―――, old diadem, xxxvii
―――, Rännelanda, Sweden, xxxviii n156
―――, Rødenes, Norway, xxxviii n156
―――, Solum, Norway, xxxviii n156
―――, suspended body, xxxvii
―――, three-nails, xxxvii, xliv
―――, Tossene, Sweden, xxxviii n156
―――, Tretten, Norway, xxxviii n156
―――, Trondheim, Norway, xxxviii n156
―――, Østsinni, Norway, xxxviii n156
crucifixion, *see* Christ
Cynegius, praetorian prefect and consul of the Eastern Empire († 388), vi
Danish
―――, loan word, xxiii
David, King of Israel and major prophet (10th c. BC)
―――, with a psaltery and a harp, vii
De altera vita, Lucas de Tuy, xxxvi
De haeretico comburendo, xx
De natiuitate domini sermo, sermon in the *NHB*, xxvii, xxviii, xxx
Denmark, viii, xlvi
Deus qui pro redemptione mundi, *see* prayer(s)
devils
―――, black, xxxii
―――, group of, xiii, xviii, xxiv
Dialogi, Gregory the Great, xii, xiii n39
Doomsday, xxvii, xxxi n133, xlii, xliii
Droitwich Priory, Worcestershire, xv
Duggall, xxvii, xxix
Duggals leizla, ix, x, xi, xii, xxi, xxiv, xxv, xxvii, xxviii, xxix, xliv, xlv, xlix
―――, prologue, ix n23

Early Middle High German
―――, verses, xxxiii, xxxiv
earth, vii, xv, xxvii
Egypt, v
―――, Upper, vi
Eilif Arnesson Kortin, Archbishop of Nidaros († 1332), xxii
elldligr himinn see emphyrium caelum
Elucidarium, Honorius Augustodunensis, xxxiv
emphyrium caelum, *see* paradise
England, xiv, xv n46, xxix n125
    fifteenth-century, xliv, xlv
    ―――, South-east, xxvii n123
    ―――, Western, xvi

English
——, craftsmanship, xxxviii
——, Parliament, xx
——, texts, ix
Établissement de Saint-Louis, Louis IX, 20 n76
Europe
——, early medieval, viii, xx n80
——, medieval, viii
——, ninth-century, viii
——, Western, vi, xvi, xxxvii
exempla, x, xi, xiv, xv, xlvii
——, moralised, ix, xlvii
Ezekiel, major prophet (6th c. BC), vii n12

Fleury, Benedictine Abbey in Saint-Benoît-sur-Loire, France, vii n11
forstoðulauss, xxiii, xlvi
Fourth Lateran Council, Rome 1215, xx, xxi
France, xiv, xv, xx
——, thirteenth-century, xliv
Franciscan
——, order, xxxvii
Frostaþingslǫg, see law(s)

Gabriel, archangel, xxvii
Garden of Eden, vii
Garden of Gethsemane, xxxv
German
——, loan word, xxiii
Germany, xiv, xv, xx
Gesta Romanorum
——, Middle English, x, xlii, xlv, xlvii
Gildisskrá, see laws
God, v, vii, xiii, xv, xvii, xviii, xxvii, xxxv, xliii, xlvi
——, the mercy of, xv
the *Gospel of Nicodemus*, xli n163
the Gospels, xxxvii
Gottskálk Keniksson, Norwegian Bishop of Hólar (15th c.), xlvi
Gregors saga byskups, xxiii n95
Gregory Barhebraeus, Syriac bishop of Gubos, Melitene, Turkey († 1286), vi n5
Gregory the Great, Doctor of the Church († 604), x, xii, xiii, xxxix
Gregory of Tours, bishop of Tours († 594), xiii n39
Guillaume Durand, Bishop of Mende (†1296), xxxvi

Handlyng Synne, Robert Mannyng, x n26
Hákon Erlingsson, Bishop of Bergen († 1342), xxii
Hákon Hákonarson, King of Norway († 1263), ix, xxi, xxii

harrowing of hell, *see* Christ
heaven, *see* paradise
hell, vi, vii, xiv, xv, xxvii, xxxi, xxxii, xli
———, abysmal pits, vii
———, Bridge of, xii, xvi
———, destruction of, xli n163
———, evil of, xxvii, xxviii
———, fire of, xxvii, xxviii
———, five locations of, xxxii
———, a great house in, xxv
———, harrowing of, xli
———, *hreinsanastaðr*, see *purgatorium*
———, hundred tongues of iron, xxvii, xxviii, xliv
———, icy location of, vii
———, infernal beasts, xiii, xvi
———, inhabitants of, vii
———, *limbus inferni*, xxxii n134
———, the misery of, xxxiv
———, the pains of, *see* punishments
———, the pit of, xxxii
———, *purgatorium*, xxxii n134, xxxii n137
———, the river of, vii, xii, xiii
———, the six locations of, xxxii
———, the tortures of, xiii, xvi, xix, xxvii, xliii
———, worms and serpents in, vii, xiv, xxv
Henry IV, King of England († 1413), xx
Historia Francorum, Gregory of Tours, xiii n39
Hólar, episcopal see, Northern Iceland, xi, xlvi
———, Cathedral funds, xlvi
———, fifteenth-century, xlv
———, the northerners at, xlvi
———, parish churches, xlvi
———, reformation of the diocese, xlvi
———, scriptorium, xlv
Homilia de assumptione Mariae, Ralph d'Escures, x
Homilia 18 *In purificatione beatae Mariae*, Bede, xxxv
Honorius of Autun, German theologian († 1154), xxxiv
Hrafn Brandsson the Old, chieftain and *lögðamaðr* in North-west Iceland († 1483), xlvi
human speech, xxvii
humanity,
———, ingratitude of, xxx
———, sins of, xliv, xlv
hundred tongues of iron, *see* hell
Hvassafellsmál, xlvi

Iceland, viii, xxi, xlvi
——, fourteenth-century, xlv
——, North-west, xii, xlvi
Icelandic
——, census, xii n35
——, codices, ix
——, diplomas, xi, xxiii, xxiv
——, false letters, xi n33
——, Homily Book (*IHB*), x, xxv, xlix
——, original letters, xi n33
——, sources, xxi
In dedicatione templi sermo, homily of the *NHB* and *IHB*, x
In die omnium sanctorum sermo, homily of the *NHB* and the *IHB*, xxx, xliv
In die sancto pasce sermo ad populum, homily of the *NHB*, x
In inventione sanctae crucis, sermon of the *NHB*, xxxv
Insular
——, homiletics, xxviii
——, homily, xxviii,
——, monastic colonies, viii
Irish
——, tradition, vii n13
Italy
——, Northern, xxix n25, xxxvii
——, Southern, vi
Isaac, patriarch, vii n14
Isaiah, major prophet (8th c. BC), vii n13

Job, patriarch, vii n14
Jacob, patriarch, vii n14
Jeremiah, major prophet (7th c. BC), vii n13
Joca monachorum, x
Jólaskrá, xxxviii
Jón Haraldsson, Jarl of Orkneys (*c.* 1231), 20 n78
Jón Vilhjálmsson Craxton, English Bishop of Hólar († 1440), xlv, xlvii
——, episcopacy, xlv
Jón Þorvaldsson, abbot of Þingeyrar († 1514), xi
Jónskirkja, Benedictine house in Bergen, Norway, xxvi n112
Judas Iscariot, disciple and betrayer of Christ, xxxix

Kenik Gottskálkson, Norwegian knight (14th c.), xlvi
Konstanz, Baden-Württemberg, Germany, viii
Latin
——, body-soul literature, xxxiv
——, books, xli
——, homilies, xxxiv
——, medieval literature, xxxvi

———, texts, ix, xxxiv, xli, xlvi
law(s)
 ———, *Borgarþingslǫg*, xxiii
 ———, Christian, xxi
 ———, *Frostaþingslǫg*, xxiii
 ———, *Gildisskrá*, xxii
 ———, *Magnus Lagabøters Norske Landslov*, xxiii
 ———, Norwegian, xxii
 ———, *Réttarbœtr Magnúss Hákonarsonar*, xxiv
 ———, Ripuarian, xxi n80
 ———, Salic, xxi n80
 ———, *Textus Roffensis*, xxi n80
Liber de homine, Ramón Llull, xxxvii
Longinus, Roman soldier who pierced Christ's side, xxxv
Lorsch, Hessen, Germany, viii n18
Lot, patriarch, vii n14
Louis IX, King of France († 1270), xx
Lucas de Tuy, Bishop of Tuy († 1249), xxxvi
Lucifer, xxvii

Magnus Lagabøters Norske Landslov, see law(s), xxiii
Maríu saga, xxxv
Marsirium, legendary King of Spain (8th c.), xxxii
Meditationes piissimae de cognitione humanae conditionis, Pseudo-Bernard, ix
Meditationes vitae Christi, Pseudo-Bonaventure, xxxvii
Micah, minor prophet (8th c. BC), vii n13
Michael, archangel, vii, xiii, xxvii, xxxii, xxxiii, xxxiv
 ———, intercessor, xv, xvi
 ———, psychopomp, xxxiv
Middle Ages, xxvii n116, xxxiv
 ———, High, xix, xx
 ———, later, xxxvii, xli, xliv, xlv, xlviii
 ———, Norse, xxi
Midlands, xvi
 ———, the West, xliv, xlv
Mikjáls saga, ix n23, xxx, xxxii, xxxiii, xxxiv, xliv
monastic vows, xxxvi
 ———, of chastity, xxxvi
 ———, of obedience, xxxvi
 ———, observance of, xxxvi
Monkwearmouth-Jarrow, double monastery in Northumbria, England, xi n32, xxv n145
the moon, vii
Munkaþverá, Benedictine monastery in Eyjafjörður, northern Iceland, xxx
Munkeliv Abbey, Benedictine Abbey in Bergen, Norway, xxvi

Nag Hammâdi
—, library, vi
New Testament
—, Apocrypha, v
Nidaros, archbishopric in Sør-Trøndelag, Norway, xxii, xlvi
Niðrstgningar saga, xli n163
Nomocanon, Gregory Barhebraeus, vi n5
Norway, viii, xlvi, xlvii
—, thirteenth-century, xxi, xxvi, xxviii, xxxvii, xxxviii
—, twelfth-century, xliii
Norwegian
—, Council of Realm, see *Riksrådet*
—, diplomas, xxi
—, Homily Book (*NHB*), x, xxii, xxvi, xxvii, xxviii, xxix, xxx, xxxv, xliv, xlix
—, laws, *see* laws
—, legal vocabulary, xlvii
—, letters, xxiii
—, manuscripts, xxii
—, sources, xxi, xxii, xxiv
Nuper huiuscemodi visionem somni, xxvi

Oddur Sigurðsson, Icelandic *varalögmaður* († 1741), xii
Odo of Cheriton, English preacher († 1246/47), x n26
Of the Death-Bed of a Profane Swearer, xlii n166
Ólafr Rögnvaldsson, Norwegian Bishop of Hólar († 1495), xlv, xlvi, xlvii
Old Danish
—, *Mass of St Gregory*, xxxix
—, *Visio Pauli*, viii
Old East Norse, viii
Old English, xxviii, xxix
Old West Norse
—, corpus, xx n79, xxi, xxxv
—, lexicon, xxi, xxviii
—, translations, ix, xlviii
ordeals
—, by fire, xx
—, by hot iron, xxi n80
—, by water, xx
—, *járnburðr*, xx
—, *ketiltak*, xx
—, *sindranda járn*, xx
Origen of Alexandria († 253/254), theologian, v, vi

Páls leizla, viii, ix, x, xi, xi, xiv, xv, xxi, xxiii, xxiv, xxvii, xxviii, xxix, xxx, xxiv, xxxv, xli, xlii, xliii, xliv, xlv, xlvi, xlvii, xlviii

Index

Páls saga postola II, xxx, xxxi, xxxii
paradise, v, vii n12, xxxi, xxxiv
    ——, ascension to, v
    ——, *festingarhiminn* see *firmamentum*
    ——, *firmamentum* 31 n133
    ——, four rivers of honey, milk, oil and wine, vii
    ——, *hvilldarstaðr*, xxxi
    ——, second heaven, xxxi
    ——, spheres of, vi
    ——, tenth heaven, vii
    ——, third heaven, v, vii, xxxi
the Passion, *see* Christ
patriarchs, vii
Paul of Tarsus
    ——, apostleship, xxxi
    ——, house in Tarsus, vi
    ——, journey to hell, vi, xxvii, xxxi
    ——, journey to paradise, v, vi, vii, xxxi
    ——, the man in Christ, v
    ——, the Revelation of, vi
    ——, visions and revelations, v n3
peccata linguae, *see* sins of the tongue
piety
    ——, popular, xxxviii
place between heaven and hell, xv
Poor Claires
    ——, order of the, xxxvii
Prague, Czech Republic, viii
prayer(s)
    ——, choral, xvi
    ——, *Deus qui pro redemptione mundi*, xxxix
    ——, Mary's prayer to Christ, xliii
    ——, Paul and Michael's intercessional, xv, xxxiv, xliiii
the profane swearer, *see* sinners
prophets, vii
Psalms, vii
    ——, Penitential, xxxix
Pseudo-Bernard, ix n25
Pseudo-Bonaventure
punishment(s)
    ——, beating, xxi
    ——, eaten alive by hounds, wolves, worms and adders, xxv
    ——, boiling in cauldrons, xx
    ——, burning at the stake, xix, xx, xliv
    ——, capital, xviii, xix, xx, xliv

——, carrying a fire and a cauldron on the shoulders, xviii, xix
——, eating of tongues, xiv
——, eating worms and serpents, vii, xiv, xxv
——, eating toads, xxv
——, everlasting, vii, xlii
——, glowing stone, xix, xx
——, *húðlát see* beating
——, immersed to the chin, xvii
——, immersed to the eyebrows, vii, xvii
——, immersed to the hands, xvii, xxxviii
——, immersed to the knees, vii
——, immersed to the lips, vii, xvii
——, immersed to the navel, vii
——, interred to the hands, xviii
——, legal, xxii, xliv
——, measure-for-measure, xvi
——, nailing of tongues, xviii, xviii n70, xx
——, public execution, xx
——, temporal, xix

Purificatio sanctae Mariae, sermon of the *IHB*, xxxv
puteus inferni see pit of hell
pyttr helvítis see puteus inferni

Ralph d'Escures, Archbishop of Canterbury († 1112), x
Ramón Llull, Franciscan writer in Mallorca († 1316), xxxvii
Randan Abbey, Auvergne, France, xiii
Randíðr, daughter of Bjarni Ólason (15th c.), xlvi
Rationale divinorum officiorum, Guillaume Durand, xxxvi, xxxvii n151
Rauðimelursyðri, Hnappadalssýsla, Iceland, xii n36
Rekaskrá, xi n33
Regensburg, Germany
——, fourteenth-century, xx
Reims, Champagne-Ardenne, France, viii n18, xxxii
Réttarbœtr Magnúss Hákonarsonar, xxiii
Riksrådet, xlvi
Ritning Bernharðs, ix
Rivers, vii
Robert Mannyng, English chronicler († 1338), x
Roland, Charlemagne's chief paladin († 788), xxxii, xxxiii
Roman
——, soldier, xii
Rome, Italy, vi n10, xxiv
Rotulus pugillaris, Augustine of Dacia, xxxii

Sainte-Chapelle, Île de la Cité, Paris, xxxvii n155
Sancti Albani, Benedictine Abbey in Selja, Norway, xxvi n112

Santa Croce in Gerusalemme, basilica in Rome, xxxiv
Satan
———, defeat of, *see* Christ
Saurbæ, Skagafjörður, Northern Iceland, xlvi
Scandinavia
———, medieval, viii, xx
Scandinavian
———, vernaculars, viii
Scotland
———, fourteenth-century, xx
———, thirteenth-century, xx
Sermo ad populum, sermon of the *NHB*, x, xxii
Sermo in purificatione sanctae Mariae, Ambrosius Autpertus, xxxv
Sermo necessaria, sermon of the *NHB*, xxii, xxx
Sermo 166 (in uigilia paschatis), William of Auvergne, xxxvi
Sermons, xv, xxx, xliv
Skálholt, episcopal see, Southern Iceland, xlvi
sinner(s)
———, betrayers of God, xviii, xx
———, blasphemers, xx, xlii
———, capital, xxxii
———, conspirators, vii
———, counterfeiters, xx
———, detractors, vii
———, dishonourers of parents, xvii
———, excommunicated, xv n47, xix, xx, xlvi
———, false swearers, xx
———, heretics, vii, xx, xxxvi, xliv
———, *illir í tungu*, xix
———, liars, xliii
———, profane swearer, xlii, xliii
———, robbers of churches, xxv
———, slayers of orphans and widows, vii
———, sorcerers, xx
———, traitors, xx
———, unbelievers, vii, xviii, xxxii n134
———, unchaste in words, xvii
———, unrepentant, xv n47, xlvii
———, usurers, vii
sin(s)
———, abuse of language, xix
———, adultery, vii, xiv
———, *bilinguium*, xix
———, *blasphemia*, xix
———, blasphemy, *see blasphemia*

———, calumny, xvii
———, *convicium*, xix
———, cursing see *maledictio*
———, earthly life of, xxvii
———, false witness, xviii, xx, xxii
———, fornication, vii
———, gluttony, vii
———, homicide, vii
———, hypocrisy, *see bilinguium*
———, incest, xiv, xlvi
———, inobservance of fasting, xvii
———, loquaciousness, *see multiloquium*
———, lust, xiv,
———, luxury, vii
———, lying, see *mendacium*
———, *maledictio*
———, *mendacium*, xix
———, *multiloquium*, xix
———, of the tongue, xviii, xix, xx, xliv
———, overdrinking, xviii
———, overeating, xviii
———, *periurium*, xix
———, perjury, *see periurium*
———, *skrǫkvitni, see* false witness
———, slander against the King, xxi
———, sorcery, vii, xx
———, theft, vii, xx n80
———, unmercifulness, xviii, xli
———, unrepentance, xv n47, xlvii
———, verbal, xix
———, witchcraft, xviii
———, wrangling, *see convicium*
soul(s)
———, a good, xxxiii, xxxiv
———, an old man's, vii
———, as an angel's bride, xxxiv
———, blessed, vii
———, of a condemned bishop, xlvii
———, of a good man, xxxiii, xxiv
———, lustful, xiv
———, sinful, xii, xiv, xv, xvi, xix, xxiv, xxv
Speculum historiale, Vincent of Beauvais, xxxii, xxxiv
the stars, vii, xxxi n133
Statuta Eilífs erkibyskups, xxii
Stave Church Dedication Homily, see *In dedicatione templi sermo*

Index

Summa de vitiis et virtutibus, William Peraldus, xix, xliv
the sun, vii, xli n163
Sunday
    ———, Easter, xliii
    ———, the Holy day of the Lord, xliii, xliii n167
    ———, respite, vii, vii n16, xv, xxxiv, xliii
Sunniulfus, abbot of Randan Abbey (6th c.)

Tarsus, city in Anatolia, Turkey, v, vi
    ———, preface, vi
tertium caelum see third heaven
text(s)
    ———, catechetical, ix, xvii
    ———, homiletic, ix, x n32, xiii, xxviii
    ———, theological, ix, xv, xxxii
    ———, moralising, ix
Textus Roffenis, *see* laws
Theodosius the Calligrapher, Byzantine emperor († 450), vi
the Trinity *see* Christ
Tristrams saga ok Ísǫndar, Brother Robert of Norway, xxi
Turpin, Archbishop of Reims († 800), xxxii, xxxiii
Twenty-first Easter homily, Gregory the Great, x
tylftardómr, xlvi

Un samedi par nuit, xxvi

Vadstena Abbey, Bridgittine Abbey, Uppland, Sweden, viii
vice(s)
    ———, capital, xix, xliv
    ———, eighth capital, xix
Viðey, Augustinian monastery in Kollafjörður, Iceland
    ———, *máldagi*, xxiii
Viðrǿða líkams ok sálar einn laugardag at kveldi, xxvi
Viðrǿða lærisveins ok meistara, x
Vincent of Beauvais, biblical scholar († *c.*1264), xxii
Virgilian cliché, *see* hundred tongues of iron
the Virgin Mary, xxxviii n157
    ———, as a beautiful woman, xlii
    ———, Annunciation, x
virtue(s)
    ———, fortitude, xxxvi
    ———, justice, xxxvi
    ———, mercifulness, xli
    ———, moderation, xxxvi
    ———, prudence, xxxvi
Visio Pauli (VP), viii, xiii, xiv, xvi, xviii, xxiv, xxv, xxvi, xxviii, xxix, xxx, xxxi, xxxii, xxxiii, xxxiv, xliii, xliv, xlvi, xlvii

———, A redaction, viii, xxxi
———, B redaction viii
———, C redaction viii
———, C1 redaction, xiii, xiv
———, C2 redaction, xiii
———, C3 redaction, xiii
———, C/spec redaction, xiii, xiv, xv, xvi
———, Old Danish, *see* Old Danish
———, Old Norse, see *Páls leizla*
Visio Tnugdali (*VT*), ix, xxiv, xxv, xxvi, xxvii, xxix
Von der Zukunft nach dem Tode, xxxiv

William of Auvergne, theologian and bishop of Paris († 1249), xxvi
William Peraldus, Archbishop of Lyon († 1271), xix
William II de Soulis, Butler of Scotland († 1321), xx n78

Þingeyrar Abbey, Benedictine Abbey in Austur-Húnavatnssýsla, Iceland, xi

Ǽfintýr (*Ǽf*), ix, x, xli, xlii, xliii, xlv, xlvii, xlix

Zachariah, minor prophet, vii n13